Tips for Teachers

By

Henry T. Conserva / Jean F. Dewees

ISBN: 1-4107-6396-X (e-book)
ISBN: 1-4107-6397-8 (Paperback)

This book is printed on acid free paper.

1st Books - rev. 10/15/03

ACKNOWLEDGMENTS

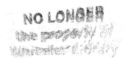

There are many people we would like to thank for their input. In all cases the desire was to make the classroom a more pleasant place for teachers and their students, thereby creating a better learning environment.

Theory is important, but most student teachers seem to want as much practical information as they can get. The people who have reviewed this work have varied experiences. Some have taught in the public schools. Some have worked in administration. Others have either taught at the college level, or worked in areas pertinent to the problems faced by many young people of today. In all cases their suggestions addressed the actual needs of the beginning teacher.

A partial listing of the people we wish thank follows:

Jeff Anderson, Teacher, Sonoma Valley High School, Sonoma, CA
Gordon Chalmers, Counselor and Teacher, McAteer High School, San Francisco, CA
Aldo Disgrazzi, Teacher, Lowell High School, and Lecturer, San Francisco State University, San Francisco, CA
Dr. Alan Fibish, Principal, Lowell High School, San Francisco, CA
Thomas F. Heafey, Teacher, McAteer High School, San Francisco, CA
Timothy Hennessey, Family Counselor
Dr. Ralph M. Jaffe, Educational Consultant
Katherine Lai, Social Studies Curriculum Specialist, SFUSD
Lisa W. Loutzenheiser, Student Teacher, San Francisco State University, CA
Duncan MacInnes, Sonoma State University, Rohnert Park, CA
Eleanor Matheu, Curriculum Coordinator, SFUSD
John S. Weir, Instructor in Photography, Diablo Valley Community College
Malcom C. Wright, Dept. Head (Social Studies), McAteer High School, San Francisco, CA

CONTENTS

PREFACE

Back in 1951, I began my student teaching assignment with my heart in my mouth. I was simply terrified. My training in teaching consisted of courses on theories of learning, educational history and the physical and psychological developmental stages of youth.

As I prepared to face a live class of energetic middle school students, I panicked. Nothing in my training had really prepared me for what I was about to face. My master teacher told me, "Sink or swim – that's the name of this game." At this point he left the classroom to me.

In some cases a student teacher will be given a choice of master teachers. If you have a choice, it would be wise to do some background research. Do they have good recommendations from previous student teachers? Do they seem to have the respect of other faculty members? Be sure to meet them all before making your choice.

I was going to be "Mr. Nice guy" and give the students considerable freedom. That was my first mistake. The students ran right over me. Students were moving around switching chairs as they pleased, leaving the room without permission and not paying close attention to what I was saying. My lack of organization made it difficult to manage the class.

Somehow I got through the day but I couldn't tell you how. I later managed to organize things and get back some control, but it was a struggle. Never again would I be so lax in dealing with a class on the first day of a new term. I would ease up on students only after I had good control of the class. Experience enlightened me on one realization; when you are dealing with secondary school students you are not dealing with adults.

Over a career in teaching spanning thirty years I have had several student teachers. They seemed to have had the same fears and anxieties I did, plus some new ones. The demands placed on teachers seem to expand continually. Teaching a subject is not enough. They are expected to be part time counselors, surrogate parents, and to participate in numerous extra curricular activities. All of this results in increasing anxieties in beginning teachers.

In my retirement years I had time to think over how I could make a useful contribution to my former profession. It occurred to me that a book of tips for teachers would fill a long-standing need that I first saw as a beginning teacher. Many of the understandings that took me years to realize could be transmitted to new teachers in a handbook or manual.

The finished book includes sections on teacher/student relations (which includes classroom management, teaching methods and student morale), teacher/parent relations, teacher to teacher relations, teacher/non-teaching staff relations, teacher/administrator relations, teacher/community relations, and some fears and concerns of beginning teachers. Advice is offered in all of these sections.

In this edition there is an addendum in which we examined the influence of computers, videos, cell phones and the Internet on teaching. Also some ideas on substitute teaching are provided.

A section on Sample Forms is also included which contains forms that should be useful to teachers facing students every day. These forms can be readily reproduced or modified to suit the individual needs of the teacher. I developed most of these forms over a period of years and found them very useful, as did some of my colleagues. Every way in which you can organize your classes will be a help as you bravely enter America's troubled but challenging public schools.

The book can be used as a guide for people presently teaching, a textbook for students of education who are training to be teachers, a primer for students who are exploring teaching as a possible career choice, or as a resource for instructors in the college education divisions (teacher training).

The information presented in this book is designed to help teachers at all grade levels, especially grades seven through twelve, by presenting ideas and suggestions that are of practical use on the job.

As in every career, "success is a journey, not a destination". We learn more from our mistakes.

PRIOR FIRST WEEK

There are many things you can do prior to the first day of class that will make that day much easier for you and for your students. Preparing a seating chart and a list of rules are two very important things to do in advance, but there are several people you need to talk to first, if they haven't already contacted you.

Don't be intimidated by all the suggestions listed in this section. Most of these tasks can be done in the course of one day. They are well worth doing. But if you are pressed for time you can do some of these things as the term progresses. However, the more you can do sooner, the easier it will be for you.

1.   Introduce yourself to the school nurse.

> Sometimes a school will provide teachers with a list of students who have special medical needs. Still, you may want to contact the nurse concerning the severity of the cases listed.
>
> If no list is provided, it is especially important to contact the school nurse who can tell you which of the students you teach have special medical needs and are in need of special consideration.
>
> Students who have hearing, vision and/or various problems of the mind and body will need special seating in the classroom. Their problems must be addressed by you in your teaching.

2.   Make contact with the head counselors or deans.

> The head counselors or deans can advise you about standards of student behavior that are upheld in the school. This will help you when you develop rules for your class, which are described in more detail in item 6 below. The class rules you develop should be shown to the head counselors or deans for comment. By cooperating with the head counselors or deans you can be more effective in your classroom management.

3.   Have a discussion with your counselors about the students.

> The past records of each student in your classes are in the hands of the school counselors. These records will usually include past grades as well as important information about the student since he or she began school. The counselors will be able to advise you in advance of potential problem situations which you may want to address in your seating arrangement or your list of rules.
>
> The more students you have, the more important it is to know all you can about each one of them.
>
> Be open minded when reading a student's past academic and/or behavioral performance file. You should witness a student's behavior before making any final judgment. People can change, for the better or for the worse, and can often surprise you with unpredictable behavior.

4.   Prepare a <u>seating chart</u>.

A good seating chart will help to prevent a great number of <u>class management problems</u> from plaguing you over the course of a school term.

The seating arrangements in your classes are best determined by you, not the students. If you allow students to pick their own seats they will develop a sense of ownership over their seats. This "territoriality factor" will make it difficult for you to make any future seating changes.

It is important that you, the teacher, tell students where they will sit from the very beginning. You may want the arrangement to be temporary the first week while students are still in flux with some students entering and others leaving the class. Also, a temporary seating arrangement will give you time to combine your own impressions of the students with the information in the school records, and make adjustments.

During this first week you may want to ask the students to speak to you at the end of class the day before you permanently assign seats. Students should tell you if they have any reasons (hearing, etc.) for sitting in front.

You have a lot to consider in the matter of making seat assignments. Having done a little research on your students already (see items 1, 2, and 3 above) you should be able to generate effective seating charts. The school nurse and counselor, having been contacted, will have advised you on special student needs. If requested, they may suggest a seating placement for those with the most unusual problems. Some students are visually disadvantaged. Others may have difficulty hearing at a distance. A few shy students who seldom speak in class might be encouraged to do so if they are seated in the front rows. Students unfamiliar with the English language may benefit by being placed close to the teacher. Highly verbal students might be better placed to the rear of the room. Some teachers engage in almost private conversations with verbally active students seated close to the teacher. Nothing could be better calculated to turn off the other students than a situation such as this.

By placing students who like to make oral contributions at the back of the class, all students get a chance to hear what's going on. An added bonus to this practice is that you, the teacher, get a better look at all your students. As you scan the class you can note who is bored and who is interested.

Romance is a wonderful thing, but be careful, in secondary school, not to seat young lovers next to each other. They may be easily distracted from the work at hand. The same holds true for talkative friends.

Having home and work telephone numbers of parents and guardians on the seating chart is a good practice. A misbehaving student can sometimes be turned around by a simple request by the teacher for him or her to verify the parents' home or work telephone number. This is an implied threat to the student that doesn't result in a direct challenge and confrontation.

Also, the phonetic spelling of the students' names should be jotted down. This will eliminate embarrassment and might even give you a few brownie points with the students. Your substitute teachers will love you for this simple addition to your seating charts.

You might consider changing the seating chart from time to time so that seating arrangements are not considered punitive by the students. However, making changes will be difficult to do if you have not been in control of the seating since the very beginning.

The main point of having a well organized seating chart is to remove the cover of anonymity behind which misbehaving students like to hide.

5.   Develop your <u>grading system</u>.

>   Work out your grading system in some detail so you can easily explain it to your students during the first days of school. Try to avoid making your grading system either too easy or too hard. Try to make it flexible enough so you don't get boxed into a corner.

>   There are good grade books available on computer programs. You might want to investigate these.

6.   Fill out a <u>temporary grade book.</u>

>   Most schools have computer print-outs of class lists. If your school doesn't, you can reproduce your class name lists, usually at the school's copy machine, and make a temporary grade book. It is better to use a temporary book, rather than none at all, while waiting for a permanent book. With this temporary book you will be ready to grade your students on the first day of school if you wish.

>   It makes an impression on the class if they see you well organized. When they observe you keeping a record of their academic and classroom behavior from the very first, they will be a little more careful about what they do in the future. When you get your permanent book, transfer all your notations from the temporary to the permanent book.

7.   Make a <u>list of rules</u> for students to follow. (See an example in the section entitled <u>Sample Forms</u>).

>   There may be a well developed school policy on standards of student behavior. If so, consider yourself lucky, and what follows may not apply to you.

>   If there is no school policy, you should be prepared to develop your own standards of student behavior in your classroom. When writing rules, be sure they are clear and specific. Avoid vague statements, such as "All students should respect each other." Instead, try for clarity. An example is "Students will speak one at a time and will not interrupt when any other person is speaking."

>   Before you meet your classes, you should work on a manageable list of rules for student behavior in your classroom. These rules might include such things as being to class on time, having necessary materials for work, not disturbing the class, not marking desks and turning in assignments on time.

>   At the time you prepare the list, you should formulate in your own mind the punishment you will enforce when the rules are broken. Frequently a private conversation with the student will suffice (<u>record the conversation, the date and the time later</u>), but you may need to consider such things as making a formal report to the appropriate head counselor or dean, a call home or a lowering of the student's citizenship grade.

>   Discuss the list with your class; you may want to make additions, deletions and modifications to your list after such a discussion. I have always found that students have many good contributions to make to any listing of rules that they will have to live by in the classroom. The sample in the Sample Forms section is a very general list that can be adapted to meet many situations.

>   Rules should be posted in the classroom where they can easily be seen by the students.

As reinforcement you may want to develop a test on these class rules to give to your students.

You may wish to show your list of rules to your colleagues and the school counselors for advice and comment before taking it to the head counselor or dean for a final review. It is important that your rules be consistent with any general school regulations.

8.   If a hall pass is not provided by your school, design one that will monitor student behavior. You may wish to use the Hall Pass form in the Sample Form section.

Some students will try to take advantage of the situation if they know they will not be held accountable for their actions. A teacher has to be especially watchful when students request to leave class. Some students seem to be continually coming up with ingenious excuses to get out of doing their assigned work in class.

Design a hall pass which will show the time a student left your class, the date, the purpose of his or her absence, the return time and the total time the student was absent from class. As your students return to class, they will turn over their hall passes to you. In recording the return time and calculating the total time each student was absent from class, you send a message to the student that says this teacher cares about what students do. Your observed act of keeping records will help to curb excessive abuses of permitted absences from your classes.

Students who abuse their privileges can be reported to the head counselors or deans. The accumulated passes will make excellent evidence for charging a student with abuse of privilege. Any necessary explanations to parents or guardians concerned will be clear, credible and uncontestable.

9.   Reproduce the Student Misbehavior Forms and the Anecdotal Record Sheets found in the Sample Forms section.

Be prepared to come down swiftly and hard on any misbehaving students right away. You must establish control over your classes as quickly as possible.

The Student Misbehavior Form should be completed when a student breaks a rule for the first time and will give you a record of the misbehavior for your files.

The Anecdotal Record Sheet will enable you to keep track of a student who misbehaves for several days in a row or over a period of time. You might consider putting down some positive comments as well as negative ones.

The students will take note of the importance you place on their behavior and usually censor themselves. After all, if you don't care what they do, or don't do, why should they?

10.   Reproduce the Unexcused Tardy Report Form in the Sample Forms section.

The Unexcused Tardy Report Form is to be handed to any tardy student who does not have a valid pass or note excusing his or her absence from class. The student will fill out the form and turn it in to you before leaving class. If the student fails to turn in the form, he or she will be considered to have been absent without an excuse, not just tardy without an excuse.

11.   Reproduce the Telephone Record Sheet in the Sample Forms section.

You may have to make a home or work telephone call to a parent or guardian in the first days of the term. It is important that you keep a record of all such phone calls immediately.

12.   Reproduce the <u>Student Profile Form</u> in the Sample Forms section.

Student profile forms can be a part of your <u>first day lesson plan</u>. These forms will allow you to obtain a tremendous amount of information about your students. You will be able to use this information to plan your course work more effectively. For example, students with a background of world travel experiences can relate these experiences to the class. An outgrowth of this exercise might be for students to write about their travels within the community, the state, the nation or the world.

Also, if the students recognize that you are using information they provided, they should react positively to you. They told you something about themselves, and you are not ignoring them.

13.   Prepare <u>lesson plans</u> for the first week of the term.

It may seem as though you're rushing things to have prepared lessons on the first day of instruction, but you should engage your students in learning activities immediately. Don't put off telling your students what you expect of them. They should be told how you want them to head their papers, study for quizzes and examinations and prepare homework assignments. They'll need to be told often and in some detail.

Having lesson plans for the first week of school will allow you to get the students started in the subject right away. They are usually quite willing to begin learning regardless of occasional protestations, so don't disappoint them.

An excellent introductory lesson is one that acquaints the students with each other. Pairs of students could interview each other and then introduce the one they interviewed to the rest of the class.

An additional bonus for you will be that while the students are working you'll have some time to complete the usual scores of forms that teachers have to fill out in the first days of a term.

14.   Have <u>contingency plans,</u> <u>fillers</u> and <u>emergency projects.</u>

Schools don't always work on a time schedule like a Swiss train. Once at my school, a special event required a 45 minute period to be extended by 20 minutes. Luckily I had been working on mini-lessons to use at the end of a class period when books were closed and students had four or five minutes of uncommitted time. I used three mini-lessons to fill the extra time.

Contingency plans are helpful to a beginning teacher who can easily miscalculate the time used in a planned lesson. It doesn't hurt to have extra material on hand to meet emergency situations. Current event games are good.

Contingency plans, fillers and emergency projects are also good for those times when you require a substitute teacher.

15.   Checking <u>your room</u> (if you have one of your own).

Before the term begins, check your room to see that all is in order. You should have a desk for each student in your class with the largest enrollment. You should have a lectern, a desk and chair for yourself, a work table, a waste paper basket, chalk, pointer, yardstick, cabinet, and pencil sharpener. Windows should be tested to make sure that they open and close correctly. Lights should be checked to see that they are not burned out.

If you find any inadequacies in the room, write them down so that you can take action on them as soon as possible.

16.   Get to know the school <u>textbook clerk</u>.

Things will go easier for you as you start a new term if you know the school textbook clerk. This clerk can tell you about supplementary textbooks that are available. The clerk can often order or borrow a set of textbooks from another school in your district if your school doesn't have a set.

The textbook clerk will be able to inform you of the school's policy regarding the care and handling of textbooks. You can get information from the textbook clerk on how to handle lost or damaged book problems with your students. In any event it is a wise policy for you to have a <u>book list</u> showing the book number and some description as to its condition beside the name of every student in your class. (See Sample Forms section for an example of such a listing.)

I used to spend some time at the beginning of a school term going over textbook matters with my students. This is the time to tell them how they can best care for their books, such as covering them, not marking them and clearly printing their names in the appropriate place in the book. It is also the time to let them know what penalties they face if the books are damaged or lost. Since textbooks are a key tool for students, the time I spent on textbook matters was worthwhile.

17.   Contact the <u>school librarian.</u>

The school librarian should be contacted before school starts. You can quickly find out about opening time and the <u>hours</u> that the library is available for student use. Your students may ask you about this on the first day, so be prepared.

Use of the library by the students should be encouraged by you in every possible way.

18.   Get to know the school <u>engineer</u>.

When I asked the engineer how the equipment worked, he proudly took me on a guided tour of the <u>heating, cooling and ventilation</u> systems.

When you get to know the school engineer you can tell him or her about the comfort level of your classroom. Proper heating, cooling and ventilation makes for better student performance in their learning activities.

19.   Locate the school <u>custodial staff</u>.

Find out the name(s) and offices of the custodial staff for future reference. You may need emergency <u>supplies and equipment</u> in a hurry. Many times on the first day of school I found I had insufficient desks for the number of students present. I contacted the school custodian immediately, only to find that others with similar requests were ahead of me. The old saying, "the early bird gets the worm" certainly applies to this problem. In the meantime, the students sat on the floor.

20.   Introduce yourself to the school <u>secretary</u>.

You can ask the secretary about any <u>forms</u> that should be filled out on the first day of school and what is required from you. This is essential if you want to minimize the trauma of your first year.

21.   Introduce yourself to the principal, but be brief.

Let the principal do the considerable amount of work he or she faces at the opening of a school term. Since he or she is your boss, a brief initial contact should be made now which can be followed up with meetings of longer duration after the term has begun.

22.   Meet with the head of your department.

Your department head is a coordinator, among other things, and is in the best position to give you the considerable amount of information that you need to know before the term begins. For example, he or she may wish you to delay passing out text books to your students, or request you to make special announcements to your classes. It is imperative that you find out about such things before you meet with your students.

DURING THE FIRST WEEK OF SCHOOL

The first week of school can often determine how smoothly the rest of the term will run. Mistakes made during the first weeks of school are very hard to correct. Your first week needs to be very well organized and many of the following tips will help you.

1.   On the first day, write your name on the board with the name and the period of the class. You may have students in the wrong class. Also pronounce your name, clearly.

2.   At the beginning of the term, send home your class schedule of the major assignments for the term and your list of rules.

   The class schedule should include a brief description of the assignment, the date the assignment will be given and the date it is due for grading. This schedule could be sent home with the student, with a tear off portion at the bottom to be signed by the parent and returned to the teacher. This can forestall later problems over the subject matter of your course that some parents might not like. This is also a way to have the student prodded by somebody besides the teacher. Make your students' parents your allies.

   When the students first arrive in your classroom, be able to present them with a copy of your list of rules (see CLASS RULES in the sample form section). Take some time to discuss the rules with the students. Make sure that they understand why the rules are important. You may wish to involve your students in making additions, deletions and modifications in your list of rules.

   After the lists have been approved by the head counselors or deans, copies of them should be sent home to the parents, signed by them and returned to you.

   Once rules are established it is vital that you take the time and trouble to enforce them. You will probably be tested by a few students to see if you have resolve. If you pass the test, you should have a fairly easy time in managing your classes from that point on.

3.   Explain your grading system to your students.

   Your grading system is best presented to the students on the first day of the term if possible. Let them know what you require for each passing grade in your grading system. You might pass out copies of your grading system to each student. There's no good reason for making students nervous about their grades.

4.   Have students complete a student profile sheet at the beginning of the term (see Sample Forms section).

   The student profile sheet should include such information as listed below. Be sure to advise your students that they do not have to complete sections of the form they wish to keep private.

      student's name
      address

          phone number
          family background information
                names of parents
                parents daytime phone numbers
                number of brothers and/or sisters
          previous schools attended
          travel experience
          favored and least favored courses taken
          hobbies
          leisure time activities
          after school work commitments
          after school activities
          memberships in clubs and organizations
          prizes and awards
          career goals
          space for information that the student wishes to share with the teacher

The completed student profile sheet will provide you with data that can help you in planning your lessons. Whenever possible, you should relate your examples illustrating a point to some personal aspect of the student or students life experiences. For example, when I was teaching Asian studies, I would often concentrate on a few selected nations within Asia. At one time I happened to have quite a few students of Filipino background and so made sure to include the Philippines as one of the Asian nations selected for intensive study.

In any discussion of careers and future job opportunities, you should include as many of the careers listed by the students as you can.

This profile can be reviewed with the parents to be sure it is up to date during a parental visit. Parents appreciate having a teacher for their children who seems to take a personal interest in them.

5.   Master the correct pronunciation of your students' <u>names</u>.

Have the students pronounce their names by getting them to stand up and introducing themselves to the class, or have <u>each</u> student write his or her name as phonetically as possible on the board so that other students, as well as you, will be able to properly pronounce every student's name. In all names, use the pronunciation the student wants.

You should start with yourself, writing your own name phonetically and explaining as you do it just what it is you are doing.

Write the phonetic spelling on your class seating charts. You may also want to do the same in your class grade book, especially for names that you consider to be difficult to pronounce.

Your substitute teachers will greatly appreciate your efforts, for mispronounced student names can cause minor classroom disturbances such as laughing or angry responses from students who are sensitive about their names.

6.   Present the students with a <u>diagnostic test</u>.

You'll be surprised how little your students seem to know if you give them a diagnostic test in the subjects you teach.

As a new teacher, you may feel that your command of the subject matter you teach is a little weak. Don't worry. A diagnostic test given to your classes will usually be enough to convince you that you really are much more knowledgeable than most of your students.

When you have become familiar with the ability level of your classes you can make up a brief diagnostic test with questions that cover some basic knowledge you feel your students should know. The results of the test will help you to develop lessons that help fill some gaps in the students' knowledge of the subjects you teach.

7.   Contact the <u>head counselors or deans</u> when major problems first occur.

It is very possible major problems will occur during the first week of school. The head counselors or deans will usually inform new teachers of their availability to help with classroom problems. Many new teachers fear contacting them about discipline problems, thinking that this will reflect poorly on their performance. Such fears are really groundless. Head counselors or deans respect teachers who spot problems when they first occur, when they are the easiest to deal with.

One bit of advice for new teachers especially is to have a record of several days of poor behavior of a particular student documented. Most head counselors or deans feel that any student can have an off day, but when poor behavior is repeated over several days, the head counselor or dean will pay attention to the teacher's report. Remember, it is the head counselor's or dean's job to get the students back on the right track.

As a young and new teacher I was quite ignorant about handling problems with girl students at the middle school where I taught. The girls' dean was a lifesaver for me. She spent some time on my education in the real world of school. Without her advice I could have had lingering and unwanted problems.

8.   <u>First impressions</u> are the most important.

The first impressions you make in the minds of the students are the most lasting ones. Therefore, you should start out strong, organized, prepared and positive. You'll get control of the class and student respect. It can be difficult to regain control once it is lost. You're not likely to have control if you start out weak, disorganized and unprepared.

9.   Get to <u>know all of your students</u> as soon as possible.

It helps you to control your classes if you quickly learn the names of your students. It is vital to be able to identify students who may need more guidance than the others in their classroom behavior. The completed student profiles form will be of some assistance to you in dealing with student problems. The importance of filling out seating charts as soon as possible cannot be over emphasized.

10.   Begin <u>classroom activities</u> as soon as possible, preferably the first day of class.

As soon as the students enter your classroom, there should be something for them to do. Your classes will be more orderly and prepared for work if you involve them in something immediately. Tasks like taking the roll are made easier when students are engaged in an activity, quiet, and in their seats.

One good assignment that keeps each student engaged in an activity as soon as he or she enters class is the journal. Every student will be required to write a few paragraphs each day on topics appropriate to the subject being taught. The students will be told that you will occasionally examine these journals and make comments upon their contents.

In my experience I found that at first students moaned and groaned at the idea of a daily writing assignment. However, as time went on, most of the students came to like the idea and some were quite enthusiastic about it. At the end of the term all the students felt that their writing skills had improved because of daily practice.

11.   Consider emphasizing lessons with practical information at least at the beginning of the term.

Many students fail to value instruction in subject matter they feel will not be useful to them. Lessons can be made more appealing to students who have this point of view by making the lesson relate to things they are involved with. Draw on their experiences.

Don't give up on teaching abstract ideas; just don't necessarily begin the term doing it. Wait until there is rapport between you and the class.

When I taught geography I started with maps of the community where the students lived. Starting from this base I was able to teach rather theoretical aspects of geography with little student resistance. If I had used an imaginary map I might have not had much success.

12.   Emphasize the concrete over the abstract in the first weeks of teaching.

Many students think in concrete terms rather than abstract ones. If you can't feel it, see it, smell it or hear it, it doesn't exist.

Audio-visual aids are one way to teach students who have difficulty working with abstract ideas. Real objects or good imitations help to give students "hands-on" experiences. Field trips are also useful in reaching students that you have difficulty reaching with printed words on paper.

13.   Experiment with caution.

Save your experimental lessons for later in the term when your class control is pretty well established. Start with assignments that are not confusing. You don't need a disaster in class to mark the beginning of your course.

I started teaching art as a beginning teacher. Was I enthusiastic! I was going to really impress the students. They were to bring old milk cartons to class to be filled with liquid plaster. After the plaster hardened, the students were to sculpt figures or abstract forms with knives brought from home. Fingers were cut and plaster dust soon covered all the halls in the school. I was unpopular with school custodians, administrators, colleagues and the students as well. I hastily ended the project which infuriated many students in the class. I spent a good deal of time that term trying to recover from my big mistake.

14.   Be quite <u>firm</u> in class control at the beginning of the school term.

> As has been said, first impressions tend to last a long time. If you start out being very strict, the students will tend to respect your authority in the classroom. As the term goes on you can ease up a little. Once your authority in the class is lost, it is very difficult to regain it.

> Don't think being easy on your students will cause them to like you. It doesn't work. In my own experience, the teachers who made me follow the rules and do the required work well had the most lasting influence on me.

15.   Continue making contacts with the <u>school librarian.</u>

> It has been said that the most important room in a school, next to the classroom, is the library. A school librarian can order books on subjects that you teach, or ones in which you have an interest. If requested to do so, school librarians can present lessons on the use of the library to your classes.

> If your school doesn't have a required orientation to the library as a part of a program for new teachers, take the initiative. You can usually ask the librarian to show you around the library. There are usually more resources than one might imagine at first sight. After an orientation session you'll be better able to direct your students to the places where they will find materials to help them in doing research on class assignments and homework.

16.   Get to know the school <u>custodial staff</u>.

> Since you want your classroom to look really good, it helps to know the custodial staff. I always found that they would gladly provide me with a few cleaning supplies, such as all purpose cleaners, papers towels and even a broom so that my students could work a little to keep the classroom clean. There is no reason to let students make a mess and overtax the custodians. The students are quite capable of cleaning up some of their own messes. I find if they have to clean up their messes, they don't make many of them.

17.   Get to know the school <u>secretary</u>.

> At times school secretaries seem to be running schools. The secretary is in a position to receive and transmit messages from and to both teaching and non-teaching staff personnel. This role as a message center communicator makes secretaries more powerful than their job description might indicate. They are among the most helpful of your support group where you teach.

> Secretaries can tell you about short cuts through the typical administrative red tape. Red tape is a characteristic of most school districts, especially those in our nation's big cities.

> Secretaries can tell you who does what and who should be contacted for information and/or service.

> Secretaries can tell you when the best time to see the principal will be. This is good to know if you are going to make any requests, or if you want a conference with him or her.

18.   Don't be anonymous to your <u>principal</u>.

> If the principal doesn't have your resume, correct the situation. If the principal knows your strengths you are more likely to get course assignments that match your academic background as well as your life experiences.

> The principal may be able to tell you about sources of money and assistance that can be used to support classroom activities, field trips, etc.

19.   Get to know your <u>colleagues</u>.

> When you know about the abilities of fellow faculty members, you can feel much more confident in arranging team teaching situations, or joint field trips for your classes.

> In getting to know your colleagues, you'll be expanding your own store of learning. I know that I learned more about teaching from conversations with my fellow teachers while eating lunch in the school cafeteria than I ever learned in college.

20.   One caution about making <u>close ties</u> with members of your <u>faculty</u> too soon.

> If you are a new teacher it might be wise for you to learn about the faculty and the relationships among the teachers before becoming too involved with them. If you become involved with members of a small clique of teachers at the school, and the values of this clique are not liked or respected by the majority of the faculty, it could be assumed you share those values by association. It's fine if you do and feel comfortable in the situation. But you may find that you did not fully realize just what you were getting into.

> The same holds true in relation to an individual teacher that you may become involved with. It's best for you to just use your common sense in such matters. The old saying "look before you leap" should guide you well.

21.   Pay attention to <u>clerical matters</u> for a happy relationship with the school clerks.

> Make sure that all the forms you must fill out are turned in complete and on time. If you do this you will get a good reputation with the school clerks. Their positive comments about you will often filter up to the principal and vice-principal who seldom see you in action teaching. Their opinions about you are often formed by seemingly small matters such as fulfilling your non-teaching responsibilities.

22.   Make your <u>classroom as visually interesting and exciting</u> as possible.

> In addition to keeping your room clean, you should decorate it with interesting materials such as posters, maps, charts, graphs, photographs and drawings. Notable quotes written on the board often provide food for thought and are a source of interpretive essays. You can get many things free from foreign government tourist offices, travel agencies and public agencies, both private and governmental. Student works' often are an excellent source of material for display. Students often observe things on the classroom walls. If only a few students get "turned-on" by something they saw on the wall, it's worth all your efforts.

> Note of caution: Don't over decorate your class to the point where it distracts students from their work or places physical obstacles to easy movement within the room.

CLASSROOM MANAGEMENT

If poor relations exist between a teacher and his or her students, almost all is lost. Students will spend so much time concentrating on what they don't like about you and your course that they will subtract from the time they should be committing to learning.

What do students want in a teacher? Fairness, commitment to the subject, consistency, good guidance, and good verbal skills could all be mentioned. But the one factor that really stands out as a must is respect. Students want to be treated with respect above all else. If you focus on this factor you'll usually be able to establish excellent relations with your students.

1.   Dress is very important in helping to create an atmosphere of respect for the teacher within the classroom.

> Don't dress like one of your students. You'll receive a lot more respect if you dress like an adult who is in charge of the classroom. Parents, administrators, visitors, non-teaching staff, parents and colleagues won't have to guess who the teacher is if you dress in a mature fashion (at least in your first years of teaching).

2.   Keep up good impressions.

> You may have made a good first impression on your students at the beginning of the term. Be sure to keep up the good impressions by not dropping your guard ever. It's very easy to lose respect in human relationships. If you dressed nicely and spoke nicely in the first week of the term, don't change.

3.   Be organized.

> You should easily be able to find all the information you need in the normal course of your activities. If you have well prepared seating charts with students' home phone numbers on them, an up to date book containing the students' grades, a schedule of major assignments, a list of rules of classroom behavior and a student profile for every student in the class you'll save yourself lots of extra hours of work.

4.   Keep good records of student classroom behavior.

> When a student breaks the rules for classroom behavior that you have presented and explained to the class, make a brief written record of the specific violation on the Misbehavior Slip (see Sample Forms section) as soon as possible while the facts are still clear in your mind. You may wish to wait and see if the violator continues in his or her misbehavior before preparing an Anecdotal Record Sheet. If you have a record of repeated offenses, the head counselor or dean can act on the matter more effectively. Also, parents can be told of specific violations and vagueness can be avoided.

5.   Keep a little social distance.

> It is important to maintain a little social distance from your students. This is especially true during the beginning weeks of a school term. You are apt to lose respect if you come on as a super friendly person or if you act like one of the kids. Most students don't appreciate this kind of behavior in a teacher. Remember, you're a role model for adult behavior as far as most of your students are concerned.

6.   Don't touch students.

>   All experienced teachers agree that, even though touching is touted now as being a good way to communicate, it is best to keep your hands off students unless it is absolutely necessary to keep them from hurting themselves or others. In a fight between students, you should try to enlist the aid of other teachers or at least try to make sure that there are witnesses to the event. Teachers are often mistakenly accused of violent behavior towards students involved in potential or actual violence. Some students have a "chip on their shoulders" and will be quick to show resentment at even the slightest touch from a teacher.
>
>   Even an innocent demonstration of fondness for a student, an arm around the shoulder or a pat on the back, can easily be misinterpreted as a sexual advance.
>
>   By not touching students you can preserve the dignity of your position and maintain the recommended degree of social distance.

7.   Be careful of students who seem to want to bond with you.

>   On occasion a student will try to bond with you. That is, a student will demonstrate a desire to make a strong personal attachment to you.
>
>   It is important that you keep a written record of what is happening between you and the student. Documentation of your conversations will be of help to you in cases where students go too far in trying to form a relationship with you. It is a good idea to notify the head counselor or dean about a problem you may be having with a student. Don't hesitate to involve the head counselor or dean in helping you with the problem. When I began teaching I had a young girl student who never seemed to leave me alone. She offered to launder my shirts. I asked the counselor for help. I'm not sure that what was done was necessarily the best solution. The girl was transferred out of my class. I must honestly say that I was personally relieved.
>
>   It is probably wise to emphasize in conversations with a student seeking a personal relationship with you that the only way you can be fair to the class is to make all rules apply equally to everyone.
>
>   Try not to be alone with any student, especially one observed to be overly attracted to you. Don't give such a student any encouragement whatever. You can be gentle but firm in declining social invitations made to you.
>
>   If you ever are alone with a student, make sure the door is open.
>
>   Contacting the head counselor or dean will be easy if you have already signaled him or her in advance that you were having a problem. A documented report about your situation will be of immense help if parents or guardians have to be involved in the matter.
>
>   Keeping your classes active and busy will help to reduce incidents of this kind of problem. Remember again to keep a little social distance between yourself and your students.

8.   Involve yourself with the entire class.

>   Don't stay in the same spot all the time. Moving is better than standing, and standing is better than sitting.

When you talk to the class, try to scan the entire class. Speak to all sections of the class and don't play favorites. By frequently looking over the whole class, you tend to spot trouble before it happens.

You want to make each student feel that you are talking to him or her. Also, you want each student to know that you find what he or she says is important. If you respond only to the best students, the others will soon lose interest and stop trying to learn and perhaps even stop doing their homework assignments. If no one cares what they think, why should they bother to think?

Research has shown that boys are called upon three or four times more often than girls. Just being aware of this should help you strike a better balance.

The students should never fear your surveillance. Walking around the class and up and down the aisles while students are doing their class work assignments lets them know two things; (1) that you know what's going in the classroom and (2) that you are available to help students individually. You should also let the students know the hours you will be available for consultation before, during and after school.

9.   Continue learning about your students.

     You will seem more like a human being to your students if you show a continuing interest in them from time to time throughout the term. You don't have to pry into their personal lives and you don't need to be overly curious. They'll be more than happy to share a good deal of what interests them in an informal conversation with you.

10.   Enforce the class rules.

     Rules lose their value if they are not enforced. If you respect class rules your students will as well. Nothing turns off students as much as a teacher who vacillates on enforcing rules. Students like security and don't care for guessing games. If students were enforcing the rules, they'd be stricter than most teachers.

11.   Follow through on what you say you'll do.

     Don't make idle statements. If you make a rule, stand behind it. If you say you will assign some work, assign it. If you say you will call the parents, call them. If you say certain oversights will be punishable, follow through with the punishment. You don't want students to think that you're a phony. However, be reasonable; punishments should not be excessive but they should be certain and unavoidable to give them the necessary credibility.

12.   Don't challenge everything that happens unless what happens is included in the list of rules.

     If you don't want to become a "burnt out" teacher, it helps if you don't challenge everything that happens in class. However, if a violation of the class rules is occurring, you must respond. If a student persists in a behavior you'd like to see ended that is not covered by the class rules - make up a new rule. Even the Constitution of the United States can be amended. Save your energy for major infractions. If you make a big thing out of all that can happen in a classroom, your career may be a short one.

13.   Don't punish the whole class for the behavior of one or a few students.

        Punishing the whole class for the misbehavior of one or a few students can give you a temporary victory and a long term defeat. About the worst thing a teacher can be in the minds of most students is to be unfair. It helps if the teacher puts himself or herself in the place of the students.

14.   Be aware of the sensitive feelings of your students.

        <u>Never</u> humiliate a misbehaving student in front of the class. First, you don't want to give up on the student. Take him or her to a private place, tell the student about the rule he or she is violating and what you intend to do about it. You want to create a situation that allows the student to come back into your classroom community in good standing. Second, the sympathy of other students can easily be aroused if they feel that you are taking an unfair advantage of one of their own.

15.   Continue being firm in controlling your classes.

        Students adjust well to routine. Firm control of your classes will be accepted by most students if you are consistent. Don't be firm one day and weak the next in maintaining classroom discipline.

16.   Communicate clearly.

        You should make sure that your writing on the blackboard can be seen and understood from all desks in your classroom. You should consider how you will be seen and heard from all desk locations. It will be helpful for you to walk to different places in the classroom to see for yourself what your writing looks like. Also, ask the students if they can read your writing and can hear you well.

        When you write comments on a student's paper, make sure that your comments are legible, grammatical and to the point. Parents often judge a teacher by a few comments made on their child's papers.

17.   Always start your classroom activities as soon as the bell rings.

        If the students know that they are expected to begin working as soon as the bell rings, they'll be more likely to get to class on time. There will be less talking and fooling around. This will help you in your control of your classes.

        It is not necessary to take roll at the beginning of the class. You can get the class started on an assignment and when they are fully engaged in their work, you can take roll.

18.   Keep them busy or they'll keep you busy.

        By keeping them busy I don't mean assigning students meaningless things to do. I mean that the teacher should have challenging lessons that engage the students and never make them feel that they are wasting their time by coming to your class. Each student reacts to a challenge in different ways based on his or her skill level, level of motivation and other factors. Different assignments might be offered to meet the varied types of students in your class. Remember, it is most difficult to keep a class busy by talking to them. It takes a rather unusual teacher to hold the attention of a mass of young people by the lecture method. The students should be doing the work and the investigation, not you.

One way of keeping students busy is through cooperative learning. Allow students to work together in pairs and small groups so that they may learn from each other.

19.   Make every class session important.

You should teach each day as though the principal of the school was sitting in on your class. It may be impossible to make each class session stimulating and meaningful to the students, but you should never stop trying.

TEACHING METHODS

Teaching methods are the tools used to get information across to students. The rich variety of methods available should make it fairly easy to keep students interested in the subject matter they are to learn. The methods you use will eventually give you a teaching style suited to your abilities and inclinations. You should find that as your career progresses both your knowledge of the subjects you teach and the ways of teaching it will develop considerably.

1.   Develop a comfortable knowledge of the subject matter.

It is necessary to have a sound knowledge of the subject matter of your courses to be an effective teacher. You can lead students to have an interest in a subject in the manner in which you might have been led yourself. A teacher who knows the subject and finds it exciting can't help but make many students wonder if there might not be something of value in what they are learning.

If you are assigned to teach a subject that you know little about, all is not lost. Get a general outline of the subject and choose a few topics to study in some depth. This will make you comfortable in at least a few sections of the course. In time, your reading and extra study will help to make you quite competent in whatever you teach. Also, don't feel shy about using the knowledge of your colleagues. They can help to give you many useful suggestions for organizing a course.

I remember when, in an emergency, I was assigned to teach a speech course. I was really rather weak in knowledge about public speaking skills and how to teach them. Two wonderful friends in the English department of the school spent some time telling me of ways to organize and teach the course. I developed an interest in the course and sponsored the school's debate club. Teaching this course became one of the most successful experiences I had in my career in education.

2.   Don't monopolize the lectern.

Don't try to do all of the talking in class. Students have a lot to say if you give them opportunities. Class discussions, panel discussions, debates, oral reports, small group reports and sessions of questioning the students are just a few of the ways that you can have students doing more than listening to the teacher ad infinitum.

When you ask a question, give the student time to think. This will allow the student to come up with a more complete answer than might otherwise have been the case.

Also, all student responses should be given respect, even though they appear to be irrelevant

3.   Don't come across to the class as a "know-it-all".

Most people, including your students, find it objectionable for a teacher to act in such a manner as to be seen as a walking encyclopedia of faultless knowledge - a "know-it-all". Content specialists are the ones most frequently guilty of this. It is an impossibility for one person to be in command of all the facts, thoughts, ideas and answers to questions that pertain to the subjects you teach, and many of your students are aware of that.

Education is a transactional process. Students learn from teachers and teachers from students. Knowing where to find information is more important than trying to stuff your head with endless facts. It is healthy for students to realize that the teacher is a student also. Learning doesn't stop at a teacher's graduation ceremony. The class should know that you and they are learning together as members of a single group.

Remember, if you don't know the answer to a question, simply say, "I don't know, but I'll get back to you". Then, once you have an answer, be sure to pass it on to the students as promised.

4.   Be a role model for speaking and writing correct English.

Students need good examples of the use of the English language. Many students in the United States today come from foreign countries. A great number of these students don't have English as their primary language. The teacher's use of correct English is more important now than ever.

It would be a good idea to tape record yourself as you read some articles from a newspaper or magazine. Play the recording to a speech or English teacher at your school to see what their reactions are and to pick up some suggestions for possible improvement.

If you can, have yourself videotaped while you are presenting a lecture. Have the camera pick up your writing on the blackboard. Is it clear? Are there any obvious problems in your written communications to students? You'll never know unless you see yourself in action as others see you.

5.   Use the egocentric nature found in most students to design lessons that will make the most of this factor.

Many students are egocentric to the extreme (adults as well). Students often exhibit a good deal of egocentric behavior in class. You can use this to advantage.

I remember when I first taught an art class in a middle school, I nearly left the job. Problem students made up the bulk of the class. Few of them wanted to do anything but make my teaching life miserable. One day I experienced a shock to my system. The assignment of the day was for students to design their own monograms. They worked diligently through the whole period. When the bell rang, quite a few of them wanted to stay on. I had to be forceful to get them to leave. Their ego involvement with the assignment taught me a lesson in motivating students.

Using student profile sheets, you should be able to relate quite a few of your assignments to personal factors in the lives of your students. One method of motivating students and involving their egos is to have them produce a product, especially one that can be easily displayed. To me, the motivation of students is a primary function of a good teacher.

6.   Make homework assignments that students can do successfully.

Homework assignments should be easily understood by the students. If a student can't grasp the assignment it won't be done. The student may just give up on homework and not even attempt to do it in the future.

One way to encourage students to do their homework is to let them begin doing it at the last few minutes of class. Problems of student comprehension of the work can be identified and clarified before they leave the room.

It is a good idea to give homework assignments that are patterned on assignments already familiar to the students in their class work. Introducing a new idea or pattern in homework is risky.

Always collect a homework paper from everyone, complete or not, and enter in your grade book promptly. Students should occasionally receive grades on their homework. Students often feel that ungraded assignments are not very important.

7.   Relate as many of your lessons to current events and to the personal experiences of students as possible.

Many students are interested in the present only. The future is the next few days and the past is the time since they were born. You have to try to use the latest news to motivate these students in their learning. Television programs, newspapers, magazines and films form the base upon which you can try to relate the present to the past and future. Since they are into television anyway, use it.

8.   Have contingency plans, fillers and emergency projects.

Contingency plans, fillers and emergency projects are recommended for the first week of school. But they will come in handy throughout the school term. You'll never be embarrassed by a shortage of teaching materials if you plan for the unexpected.

9.   Liven up your classroom presentations with lesson plans from your colleagues, your professional organizations or from anyone.

I remember a line from a comic song lyric that goes "plagiarize, let no one else's work evade your eyes". This is a good guide to your acquisition of lesson plan ideas. You'll find lesson plans everywhere you look. Your colleagues, your professional organizations, educational journals, and the daily newspaper are just a few good sources for you to use, as well as the bibliography in the back of this book.

10.   Develop a classroom library for easy location of information.

A classroom library might consist of a few key reference materials in the subjects that you teach. A cautionary note; some of these items might be lost or stolen.

When students ask those inevitable questions you can't answer, you can look up most of the answers quickly in your reference works. If no answers are found you can tell the student that you'll do research later or you may direct the students to the library to do the work and report his or her findings to the class.

Students will get into the habit of using reference works by the example you set. Also, you won't be seen as a "know-it-all" if you show the students that you have to look up answers to questions just like they do.

Students can be told that they will have access to these books at any time they want as long as they do not disturb you or the class.

11.   Be careful in having students express themselves orally in class.

Asking students to express themselves orally in front of their classmates can be playing with fire. If the topics under discussion are fairly neutral, things will probably be just fine. But if you lead students into areas such as politics, race, sex relations or social class differences you could get into some serious problems. It might be best to have students express their opinions on emotionally charged subjects in writing to stave off any possible embarrassment or worse.

12.   Develop the students' thinking skills by asking them a variety of questions.

Educators from Socrates' time (and I suspect well before) down to the present have recognized that a fundamental way to develop the thinking skills of students is to ask them to struggle with questions that go beyond the simple recall of facts. However, there is no need to embarrass or antagonize the students.

We, as teachers, should probably spend much more time working on formulating good questions than we do. Effective questions have always led to even more questions as well as great advances in all fields of knowledge. I think that the art of questioning has been somewhat neglected at all levels of education. Far too many questions call for nothing more than factual information which the student has hopefully memorized for recall on demand. This kind of questioning certainly has its place in the classroom, especially since many of the tests students must take call for factual information. But if we are truly committed to educating a person, we need to develop questions designed to do more than stimulate student recall. We must help students to comprehend facts, apply facts, analyze facts, synthesize facts and evaluate facts, all without damaging the sensitive egos of youth.

Types of Questions:

A. Knowledge Questions:

The question that asks for a recall of facts is the most common found in classroom use. Knowledge of people, places and things is vital to students who must answer questions of this type constantly. Since most tests test for a command of facts, you must include many questions of this type in any teaching strategy.

e.g.   1.   What is the capital of Syria?
        2.   Water boils at what degree Fahrenheit at sea level?
        3.   Who wrote Hamlet?

B. Comprehension Questions:

Questions of this type go beyond testing students' command of facts. We need to know if students really understand the facts they have memorized. The ability to define a term, to understand and explain a concept and to identify cause and effect relationships, are just a few of the factors involved in students' comprehension of facts.

e.g.,   1.   How has Communism changed life in China?
        2.   What is a nation?
        3.   What is photosynthesis?

C. <u>Application Questions</u>:

Application questions are practical questions that require students to show that they can use facts to solve a variety of problems. In a way, application questions are a test of the students' comprehension of facts. These questions encourage students to make connections among many related items and specifically to make useful analogies. Questions like these call upon students to take some risks, and to venture into the realm of speculation. The risks are well worth taking.

e.g.,   1.   The road distance between San Francisco and Los Angeles is about 400 miles. What is the distance in kilometers?
          2.   How does gravity effect our launching of space vehicles?
          3.   Show how the use of emotionally charged words can slant the news.

D. <u>Analysis Questions</u>:

These questions call for students to separate a whole into its constituent parts. Historians are constantly trying to analyze periods of human history in order to identify the factors that influence human events at any particular time and place. The ability to analyze is of great value to anyone who writes essays or compositions. There are innumerable concepts and ideas that include many factors, each of which could be a subject for discussion.

e.g.,   1.   What are the factors that influence climate?
          2.   What were the causes of the Civil War?
          3.   What are the types of business organization?

E. <u>Synthesis Questions</u>:

Questions of this type call for students to combine separate elements to form a whole. All the great thinkers in human history have been synthesizers. Confucius placed various ideas together to provide a plan for living that has lasted for thousands of years. Karl Marx used his ability to synthesize ideas and created an ideology we call Marxian Socialism or communism. The famous Constitution of the United States is a perfect example of political ideas combined to form a whole. Students can, in a small way, synthesize ideas to form a concept and in so doing, follow the same process that was used by history's greatest minds.

e.g.,   1.   What would be an ideal location for a new city in your state?
          2.   Describe an ideal society for the year 2010 A.D.
          3.   How would you improve the public schools in your community?

F. <u>Evaluation Questions</u>:

This type of question calls for the student to examine a question or a fact and then go on to make a judgment. Almost everyone has an opinion on just about everything until called upon in class to offer one. Then the teacher often finds an uncharacteristic silence. To evaluate is a high risk venture. A student may think, "What if my opinion offends the teacher or my fellow classmates?" The student will use silence as a defense mechanism. It may be best to ask for written responses to evaluation questions that are likely to stir up strong emotions in the class.

e.g.   1.   What are the best places in the world for human habitation?
         2.   Who ranks first in importance and influence among all the presidents we have had?
         3.   Who would you rank as America's most influential artist?

13.   Turn the student into a teacher whenever possible.

Many students have expectations of low achievement in their mental baggage. This condition can be a result of little or no adult support or encouragement for the student to develop natural skills and abilities. Inadequate opportunities to succeed in the class work can also be a factor.

I have had some success helping students to overcome bad feelings about their capabilities by making the student the expert. You can look through a student's profile sheet to find something unique and/or interesting about experiences they have had, jobs they have performed, awards they have received or goals that they are working for. Get them to share at least one thing with you and the class. Stress that you and the other students are learning something of value.

14.   Design projects that encourage students to use their own hands in making something.

Many students value action over passivity. Not every student learns best by reading a textbook. Having them make a paper mache relief map of the state can impart geographical knowledge to students that words will never quite match. Posters or collages can do the same thing.

Time lines can give students a feeling for chronology that the reading of dates will never provide.

15.   Let the students do the work.

As a teacher you should exhaust your students, not yourself. Youthful energy is best channeled into constructive endeavors. Students should be doing the research, locating the information, reading and writing. Having students read aloud in class can be a useful technique. I was really surprised how students in the lower grades enjoyed this. It presented the student with an opportunity to explain the section he or she read. You can lecture from time to time but you should ration yourself. If students get into good work patterns you'll have time for planning lessons and grading papers.

16.   Use the capabilities of your bright students.

Bright students often suffer from classroom boredom. Try giving them independent work assignments. Let them do research on selected topics using the resources of the school library. You may wish to get ideas from them on how they might like to approach the study of the subject you're teaching them.

You can enlist these students to help teach slower students in small group settings. Placement of your bright students at the rear of the class can help to encourage discussion among other students and you. On the other hand, if the bright students are sitting in the front, the rest of the class can easily feel left out of what's going on. Also, while you're engrossed in conversing with those in front, those in back may be doing things you are not aware of.

Avoid loading up these bright students with extra work. Just make the work you assign them to do challenging.

17.   Have every student turn in a homework paper, completed or not.

Even if a student has not done his or her homework assignment, insist that each student turn in a paper. The paper may only have the student's name, the day's date and the title of the assignment on the page. Return the completed homework assignment papers to your students and retain the others.

As a teaching practice use some excellent examples of well done assignments, minus the name of the student who did the work, to show students how homework assignments should be done.

One thing is sure, in having everyone in the class turn in a paper, you'll have a record of what your students have done and what they have not done. Imagine the look on the faces of parents when you place four or five blank homework assignments in front of them alongside properly completed ones. Arguments about the student's performance will seldom be forthcoming.

Students who skip homework assignments are usually quick to realize that you are building up a damaging record against them. Some students may be motivated to do their assignments as a result of your concern about what they do and don't do. Occasional grading of homework assignments will reinforce this attitude.

Another plus in this practice is that all students see papers being turned in. The students doing their homework won't feel like a group of outcasts among their peers. Students won't really know how many or how few class members did the homework. All of these realizations should ensure a respectable number of completed homework assignments being turned in to you.

18.   Encourage students to turn in clearly written work assignments.

Students need to be encouraged to think before they write. I circle "student cross-outs" and several of these on a paper will require the student to rewrite the paper. I also circle phrases that I cannot read. Several of these on a paper will require the student to do a rewrite. Having to rewrite their papers motivates students to think more carefully before they commit pen to paper.

19.   Put variety into your daily teaching when possible.

Many students have a brief attention span for what is going on in class. You can't speak too long on one subject without losing some students. Variety in subject matter and teaching activities can fight the effects of inattention among students.

20.   Lessons don't always have to be serious and somber.

Most students value fun and entertainment and this can be used to the teacher's advantage. Lessons can be fun without losing their educational effectiveness. Puzzles, games and dramatic skits can be incorporated into many lessons.

I used to have students volunteer to represent famous people. They had to research their chosen personalities for a few days. Meanwhile, the other students worked on a question list to use in interviewing famous people. The students who took the parts of various famous people were then interviewed by the class. It was entertaining but the students learned quite a bit about many key figures in history.

One of my most joyous experiences happened when my class, <u>with the approval of school administrators,</u> put on an ethnic foods day at lunch time. Each ethnic group represented in the class worked on the project. The project was initially my idea, but they took the ball and ran with it. They prepared the food at home and sold the meals in the school yard at noon. There was a great deal of cooperation among and between the groups.

21.   Be consistent in your practices in the classroom. Routine provides security for many students.

Establish a routine and stick with it. Students don't like guessing games. If you tell them you'll take them to the library every Wednesday and that Friday's will be test days, don't upset them too often by changing the library or test days. Students want to know what's coming at them. They feel more relaxed with routine than with a constantly changing series of classroom practices.

When I act as a substitute teacher I find that the students will usually lead me into the routine activities of the class. True, they do like a different teaching style for a while, but if they don't return to their routine activities soon, they begin to feel uncomfortable.

22.   Repetition is not a bad idea.

Don't be afraid to repeat facts. You can repeat an idea without sounding like a stuck record. Say the same thing using different words. You may have to do this three or more times before some of your students begin to grasp what you are saying. Every chance you get to have students review what they have been learning should be seen as an opportunity to be effective. Students should write summaries or synopses of the chapters in their textbook.

Repetition and carefully reviewing work helps students to retain information. A friend of mine in high school was a self-proclaimed rebel. He couldn't be forced to study by some "dumb" teacher! He kept to his word and all but went to sleep in the U.S. History class. The teacher was big on repetition and review. My friend couldn't shut out the teacher, try as he would, and learned enough in spite of himself to get an above average grade in the final examination for the course. The teacher flunked him!

23.   Use a classroom calendar.

Don't keep the students in the dark as to what is expected from them. You can write on the blackboard "Coming Events" and list such things as library days, due dates for assignments, test dates, the dates you'll have a substitute teacher, etc. Keep the list updated and it will help to provide structure and security for the students.

24.   Be consistent in your beliefs in relation to your behavior.

Students really tend to look up to teachers. They expect them to be rather exceptional. "Do as I say but not as I do" won't work. Students have x-ray vision. They seemingly can see right through you.

25.   Encourage your students to work together.

> Group work is a good way to get your students to interact with each other. Students really do teach each other quite a bit. In law school especially, students often form study groups. There's no reason why this can't be tried in certain secondary school courses.

26.   Try to get bias and prejudice out of your teaching.

> Your mission as a teacher is not to indoctrinate your students with your pet ideas. Your mission is to try to educate your students. This means that you make a real effort to present all sides of an issue fairly. Your real feelings on a controversial issue need not be revealed to your students.
>
> If your biases and prejudices come out too clearly you'll usually find out. Students will challenge you and your peers will get to you. You personally may think that you are unbiased and unprejudiced in all areas. This would be truly unusual if not impossible.
>
> One way to handle biases and prejudices is to list them and then try to list reasons in support of each one and reasons not to support each one. It will be painful but it will be a worthwhile exercise.

27.   Learn speed-reading and scanning skills.

> You'll be faced with a lot of written work to correct and examine in almost every subject you'll teach. A speed-reading course might help you to deal with the paper load.
>
> If you develop your skill in scanning material you won't be going to bed at 2:00 A.M. with bloodshot eyes.

STUDENT MORALE

One of the most important factors in students' ability to learn is how they feel about themselves. If you can build self esteem in students, you'll be motivating them to succeed.

I remember in my army experiences how a confused, bewildered, and somewhat frightened group of young men, myself one of them, were transformed into a good fighting unit. Our trainers had high expectations for our performance and we had to repeat exercises until we met their standards; failure was unthinkable and unacceptable. When we did things wrong, we heard about it, but when we did things well, we also heard about it, and that is what made the difference. We grew in self-confidence and overcame our fears. I feel that what was true in the army can apply to the school room. Good student morale should be given top priority in our teaching.

1.   Help to give students confidence in themselves.

   When you introduce an assignment or topic to the class, make sure that it is logically organized and contains vocabulary appropriate to the ability level of the class. Tell the students that the assignment or topic is easy to understand.

   Most people tend to underrate their abilities and your students are no exception. Reinforce the students' confidence in themselves by praising them when they show comprehension of the work. An honestly deserved compliment will often motivate a student to strive more energetically in his or her work.

   I remember one of my math teachers in middle school. She said, "We're going to do a problem in algebra today". She had everyone do a fairly complex problem. She had very clear steps to take in solving the problem. Every student was able to get the correct answer. Then she announced to the class, "You've all done a problem in algebra. If you can do this one you don't have to be afraid of the subject." Her psychology worked for me and my classmates.

   Students should be reminded that each one of them possesses the greatest and most complex computer ever developed, the human mind.

2.   Praise your students when they deserve it.

   Almost all people like recognition by others. Students are no exception. Napoleon said that if you give a man a medal he'll die for it. Students can be motivated by praise. They can lose motivation by a lack of it. You can praise students for performing a task well, coming up with a stimulating idea, bringing something interesting to class or changing unsatisfactory behavior to satisfactory behavior.

3.   Be a good listener.

   Give your students some feedback so they'll know that you heard them. Nothing turns a student off more than the feeling that the teacher is not paying any attention to what he or she has said. When you say things such as "Jane had a great idea yesterday. I thought about it a lot after class.", Jane will pick up on your remarks. She'll be more willing to share her ideas with you and the class in future discussions. Other students will feel that they can get recognition too.

4.   Give encouragement to shy students.

> Don't always call on the same eager students who always seem to have their hands up. Other students less bold will give up trying to participate in oral class work and depend on the question answering kids to do all the work. It might be helpful to have each student's name on a 3"x 5" card and use the cards to record the students oral progress in class. By regularly going through all the cards, each student will eventually be called upon to make an oral response to a question.

> Several things can be done to bring a shy child out of his or her shell. A shy student's remarks should seldom be negatively criticized. Any reasonable response by a shy student to a question should be encouraged.

> You can provide a safety net for all students, not just shy ones, by allowing them to say the word "pass" if, for any reason, they do not want to respond to a question. Students should not be allowed to abuse this privilege, and you may wish to say something about this in your list of class rules.

> I tell my students that their brains resembled the chips in a computer. All the chips working together allows the computer to solve difficult problems. Students should never remove their chips from the class computer.

5.   Reinforce the students' identification with their respective ethnic groups.

> Speak positively about the ethnic groups represented by the students in your classes whenever possible. The grade counselor might be able to give you information on students from foreign countries. You might want to read about any ethnic groups with which you are not familiar. You might even consider letting the students teach you something about their ethnic groups. For example, you can have students tell jokes that are funny in their homeland (they may not be funny to Americans and this should be stated in advance of the exercise). Depending upon the maturity level of the class, this could be a sure morale booster for students from foreign lands who are newcomers to the United States.

6.   Keep your students informed about their class grades.

> No grade should be a surprise. Students should know exactly where they stand at any given time regarding their grades in your class. You should have a system of grading, perhaps using a point system, by which the students could average out their own grades. This way you won't be constantly pestered by students saying, "What's my grade"?

> It bears repeating to tell the students that you do not give them grades, they earn them. To be able to make a remark such as this, you have to be sure your grading system is as objective as possible.

7.   Return graded work to the students promptly.

> You lose a lot of the educational value of an assignment if you fail to return it to the students within a reasonable amount of time. I'll bet that when you were a student you appreciated a teacher who returned the graded assignment to you promptly, especially tests and quizzes.

8. Let your students contribute to your course planning.

If students are given options on what you should stress in the course, they'll feel important. They'll feel that their ideas count for something. You just might find that the students become more motivated in doing their assignments than they would have otherwise.

Many students would enjoy coming up with their own ideas for projects and other learning activities, such as field trips, classroom skits, creative use of television, etc.

9. Keep the students informed.

Students should know such things as when assignments are due, what the directions are for each assignment, who can help them in their work and what to do if they run into any problems. Students need repeated reminders of such things as due dates on assignments and steps to be taken for completing major projects. A class bulletin board containing important information for your classes is a good idea at any grade level. Never give students an excuse for not doing their work.

10. Be courteous and respect your students' feelings.

It doesn't hurt if you use such terms as "thank you", "if you please", and "ladies and gentlemen" on occasion. If students are treated in a courteous manner they will think better about themselves. Don't put a student down by making remarks such as, "That's a really dumb answer!", "What a crazy question!" or "Can't you come up with an idea better than that?" The best rule to follow in this is to put yourself in the student's place. Courteous behavior will help to bring a student out of his or her ego protecting shell. Discourteous behavior will have just the opposite effect.

11. Talk to the students as though you are first among equals.

Speak to your students as if they were as interested and as excited about the subject matter in the course as you are. If you are condescending in your manner, the students will quickly feel that you are putting them down. If you suddenly start talking at a very slow pace and using very simple words, you'll turn them off. If you think that they'll be bored by the subject matter, they probably will be.

12. Be human.

There's nothing wrong with letting your students know that you're a human being. There's little to be gained from trying to show the class that you're Mr., Ms. or Mrs. perfect, or Mr., Ms. or Mrs. powerful. It strains students if they think that you are a teaching machine without feelings, especially good feelings, about them. You should be capable of saying "I don't know" when you are asked a question. The thing to do is to say that you'll look up the answer or, better yet, look up the answer with the student. Let them know that learning is a lifelong pursuit and that you are both a teacher and a student yourself.

13. Show an interest in student activities outside of the classroom.

Be seen by your students at school functions; go to a play, volunteer to supervise a dance, attend a game, sponsor a club, etc. Students really do appreciate it when you show an interest in their activities outside of class.

14.   Be fair in all your dealings with your students.

> In enforcing class rules, you should treat all students alike. You must be prepared to do for all what you do for one. In any student listing of qualities appreciated in a teacher, students universally list fairness at or near the top.

15.   Relate to the whole class.

> Don't relate to a few students exclusively. Each student needs to feel that he or she exists in the mind of the teacher. Youthful egos are very easily bruised. You can relate better to the whole class by following an earlier tip and having 3"x5" cards of all the students to make sure that you call on all of them. However, be careful not to make it mechanical. e.g., don't make a major production of bringing out a file box. Don't always follow the same order of call. Don't spend time marking the cards while students are talking. Remember your thoughts about the students' performances and mark the cards as soon as possible later. Don't have the same students doing your errands for you. Don't make comparisons between one group of students and the rest of the class in a way that divides the class into warring sections. You want to keep all the students together as members of one group.

16.   Help to break down gender stereotypes.

> Girls are perfectly capable of carrying books. Girls can push a television set through the halls of a school just as well as the boys can. By only choosing boys to do tasks requiring some strength and by only choosing girls to do the "lightweight" tasks, you are putting out messages to both boys and girls that they are in certain ways inferior or not capable.

> Don't leave students with the impression that all human accomplishments were the work of men or for that matter of women. Try to keep a balance in your teaching about humans and their activities.

17.   Develop a sense of humor.

> This is not necessary if you are only going to teach for a week and then go into some other line of work. But if you are thinking of making teaching a long term career, you'd better learn to laugh at many of the things that will inevitably happen to you. Your good health demands that you develop a sense of humor. You'll seem like a flesh and blood person to both your colleagues and your students if you do.

18.   Keep up your morale and you'll help student morale as well.

> You need to have relaxation and recreation for yourself to keep up your morale in teaching, one of the most demanding careers known. You can influence students by your emotions and moods. If you are positive, secure and content, the students will pick up on that and they may well feel better themselves.

TEACHER/PARENT RELATIONS

Good teacher/parent relations are an essential backdrop to a student's good learning experience. Parents can be your allies working toward a common goal - that of educating youth. In a way, parents are the most important teachers in a student's life. Traditionally, the mother has taught the child the most basic and important lessons of life; how to speak, how to walk, how to deal with others in social situations, etc.

Teacher/parent relations are in a state of change. Many children come from single parent families where the burdens of child rearing are tremendous. Today's students need all the help they can get from as many adults as possible.

1.   Keep open the lines of communication with parents.

You've already sent home a schedule of major assignments for the term and the class rules. This is an excellent beginning of what should be a continuous process of communication between you and the parents of your students. A great number of our inter personal problems can be blamed on poor communication.

When you get a phone message from a parent, call as soon as possible.

2.   Before meeting a parent, quickly read over the student profile of their child or children.

A student profile was completed by each student at the beginning of the term. This profile can be reviewed with the parents to be sure it is up to date. The parents may be able to expand the information in the profile considerably. This display of interest in the student will register with parents in a positive way.

3.   Encourage parents or guardians to look over their children's homework.

This is one sure way that parents can determine how well their children are doing in class. You might find it helpful to keep a few <u>copies</u> of the actual class work assignments completed by the students to show parents. Compositions are especially useful to save for they show how well the student communicates in writing, which is a key academic skill.

It has been suggested that parents receive a breakdown of grades for the marking period, in addition to report card grades. This is based on the idea that one grade on a report card under a caption such as "English" does not reveal how well the student has done in reading, writing, speaking, etc. The student or the teacher could prepare an assignment file with the assignment titles and grades logged in

4.   Keep good and complete records on your students' academic work and classroom behavior.

You should keep complete narrative statements on each student. Letter grades really do not communicate what many parents want to know about their child's achievements. Your records should indicate how well a student reads, speaks and writes in the English language and should include specific examples of the student's classroom behavior. You should make your notes while the activity is still fresh on your mind.

For example, being able to tell a parent that their child has a limited vocabulary, stumbles over many words, and has a weak voice is more meaningful than telling them their child is an average reader.

Being able to tell a parent that their child disrupts the class frequently, comes late to class and leaves the textbook in the locker is more meaningful than telling them their child's class behavior is below average.

5.   Do not be shy in calling the parents of your students by phone when necessary.

> A direct communication with parents will show them that you care. If you are concerned about a student's behavior, let the parents know. They usually will appreciate your concern. You'll gain a potential source of assistance. Keep a record of your phone call, the date, time, who you talked with and a summary of what was said. If you have difficulty reaching a parent by phone, you might want to keep a record of the number, dates and times of your attempted calls.

6.   Be informed of your students' complete ethnic background.

> The maiden name of the mother will often help to identify her ethnic background. Our patriarchal naming system can bury a mother's last name. Children in our society are basically associated with the father's last name. A child with a last name such as Rossi gets the Italian label. His or her mother's last name may be a Russian, Polish or Chinese one but these labels will generally not be applied to the student. If you organize any ethnic awareness activities, both sides of a student's family should be considered. Most parents will appreciate a teacher's sensitivity in this matter.

7.   You might consider joining the Parent Teacher Association (PTA) in your school.

> Better relations with parents are often essential to the success of a teacher. Troubles and difficulties can be headed off before things get out of hand if you have some backing and support from parents. You can learn about some of the things that are troubling your students that will help you in understanding them better.

TEACHER-TO-TEACHER RELATIONS

It has been said that "No man is an island" and this is especially true of teachers. Your colleagues can enrich your teaching skills immeasurably. The interaction of mind is one way in which creative and innovative teaching ideas can be born. You are in a profession loaded with dedicated people who share many of your hopes, thoughts and values. It would be criminal and foolish to ignore colleagues who could help you so much in doing a better job in your chosen profession. An added thought, in getting help from your colleagues it is well to remember that you will be helping them as well.

1.   Get to know your colleagues.

> Learn as much as you can about the general and special abilities of the members of the teaching staff at your school.

> When you make friends with enthusiastic and dedicated teachers, you pick up energy from them. They are good role models for you. Remember, there is real joy in teaching. The rewards may be intangible but they can sustain you throughout your career. One of the best contributions you can make to society is to pass on your enthusiasm for teaching and learning to your students.

> I have always felt a little sad that a truly great and unusual teacher always seemed to have a limited audience. The students lucky enough to get into such a teacher's class received truly exceptional educational experiences, while a high percentage of the rest of the student body did not. One solution for a problem of this sort is for you to approach selectively other teachers about exchanging classes for a period, a day, or longer. By teachers covering each other's classes, they can at least double the number of students who can learn from a new perspective other than the one held by their regular teacher.

2.   Participate in faculty social events and extra-curricular activities.

> A good way to get others to know you is to let yourself be known. Faculty social events are an opportunity for you to make contacts. You'll need all the friends you can make before you wind up at your retirement dinner!

> I've never known a teacher who didn't benefit from the support and criticism of a good many of his or her colleagues from time to time. And there's a surprise in participating in social activities centered around the school, you may get to like them. I remember the time I was persuaded to join a faculty group in putting on a dinner program for the parents of our students. When the group found out that my last name was Italian, guess what the menu became? That's right, spaghetti! I never made so much spaghetti in all my life, but it was tasty. Local business people supplied wine and crunchy bread for the occasion. The whole event was great fun, and I got applause from the parents for my efforts.

3.   Don't make your substitute teacher suffer.

> Have well constructed lessons available for the substitute. Lessons that your substitute can succeed with are essential. Make sure that your seating charts and student information forms are up to date and easily accessible to the substitute.

It would be a good idea for you at the beginning of the term to appoint class monitors in each of your classes to assist the substitute in taking roll, to help in locating lessons and materials and to be generally helpful. Taking these steps will also make things a little easier for you when you return to your classes.

When you can't be present to teach your classes, pity the poor substitute. You certainly can remember how substitutes were treated by students at the schools you attended.

TEACHER AND NON-TEACHING STAFF RELATIONS

The non-teaching staff is a body of support personnel who are to make the job of educating the children of the community efficient and easy for you. Cooperating with them is a wise policy. In a modern school it is impossible to be a master of all trades. We need specialists to get the job of education done. You really wouldn't want to teach in a school that didn't have a high quality non-teaching support staff.

1.   The <u>school secretary</u>.

All through the term you'll have reasons to relate to the school secretary. He or she will have countless forms for you to fill out and papers to turn in. The secretary can do favors for you in many ways. For example, if you want a specific substitute teacher, the secretary can help out.

Remember that this person may have to work in a zone of constant cross-fire, i.e., under pressure most of the time.

It won't hurt to show your appreciation for all the favors a secretary can do for you. Express your thanks for a job well done.

2.   The <u>counselors</u>.

Counselors are in possession of more intimate details of your students' lives than anyone else at your school. They hear the things that students may not tell their teachers. I found that counselors could tell me in advance about certain students who may have needed a little extra attention from me to keep things running smoothly in my classes.

The past records of each student in your classes are in the hands of the school counselors. They are the ones who can help you with students who seem to be problems for you.

Whenever I had an official school visit from a parent pertaining to a serious problem with the student, I found it most helpful to have the counselor present to help me through the meeting. One counselor was able to support my description of a certain student's behavior by referring to similar descriptions from other teachers.

Counselors do more than take care of problems; they inform students of opportunities for further education or career training. You can and should inform the counselors about outstanding students who may qualify for scholarships. Counselors are always pleased to receive some feedback on students from the teachers.

For all of these reasons it is important for you to make contact with the counselors on a regular basis throughout the term.

3.   The <u>school librarian</u>.

Your school librarian is one of your support personnel that contribute mightily to the education of students. The librarian promotes the reading of both current literature and the classics. He or she will often walk students through assignments, helping them find the necessary reference works to help them complete their projects.

Even though the school librarian is listed as a non-teaching staff member, he or she definitely has a teaching function. Most librarians will be quite happy to provide formal instruction on the use of the library to classes of students.

Don't abandon your classes when you take them to the library. Help the librarian in maintaining order in the library and the librarian will give you the support you need for effective teaching.

Be sure to return a few favors to the librarian. You should always tell the librarian about any lessons or homework assignments that are going to involve the use of the library so that he or she will be able to prepare for the students.

4.   The <u>school nurse</u>.

The school nurse can be helpful to you in many ways. The nurse can inform you of any new medical problems involving any of your students. You can learn to deal with some medical emergencies in your classroom by asking for some instruction from the nurse.

I remember one term in which emergency kits were put in each teacher's box with some basic instructions. I questioned the school nurse, and she told me about one of my student's epileptic seizures. The nurse instructed me in how to handle the student and how to use some of the medical equipment in the kit if a seizure occurred. I never thought that I would have to deal with such a problem. Surprise! The student had a seizure in my class and I was able to handle things fairly well. Thanks to the school nurse.

5.   The <u>school food service personnel</u>.

You can learn a lot from a few brief conversations with the school's food service personnel. For one thing, and this is a plus for you, they can tell you what food is pleasing to adults and what food is not. Armed with this information, you can be a friend to your stomach at school.

They can tell you quite a bit about your students' "out of class" behavior. They see a side of your students that you may never really notice.

6.   The <u>school custodial staff</u>.

Keeping in communication with the school custodial staff will help you to keep your classroom presentable. The custodians might be able to inform you of the messiness of your students. A few clean up sessions after school will usually correct this problem.

The custodians frequently will be able to give you cleaning supplies that the students can use to add a sparkle to your classroom on special occasions, such as parents' night.

A note of caution; be careful with the use of chemicals, especially sprays.

7.   The <u>school engineer</u>.

You never know when things will go haywire with heating and ventilation in your room. Don't fail to keep up contacts with the school engineer. They often times appreciate the feed back that teachers can give them so that fine adjustments to complex systems can be made.

8.   The <u>school textbook clerk</u>.

        In most schools the school textbook clerk, besides handling textbooks, is in charge of audio-visual equipment. By all means, keep up your contacts with this clerk. He or she can tell you what films are good and how you can cut through red tape to get what you want. It helps if you know the textbook clerk's procedures.

9.   The <u>school clerks</u>.

        Continue to cooperate with the school clerks. Make sure that all the forms you must fill out are turned in complete and on time. Don't hassle them - they are just following orders. If there is something going on in school you don't like, get to the source instead of taking it out on the clerks.

10.   Use the <u>non-teaching staff</u> as a resource for your students.

        Non-teaching staff members can be used as interviewees by your students. If you get permission from these people in advance, you can prepare your students to interview them in a proper manner. I wouldn't do this very often, but whenever I assigned interviews of this kind they were very successful. Both adults and students learned a good deal about each other.

TEACHER/ADMINISTRATOR (Principal and Vice Principal) RELATIONS

Good administrators are not your enemies. They want to have a school with a good reputation as much as you do. One way a school gets a good reputation is to have an outstanding core of teachers. Administrators know this and so they don't want you to fail, but to succeed. They have a vested interest in a superior performance from you. A good school is run on a team system. With administrators and teachers cooperating, your job will be pleasurable and rewarding.

1.   Volunteer for an out of class activity you want to sponsor.

As a new teacher you may be asked by the principal to sponsor any number of extra-curricular activities. Make a pre-emptive strike by contacting the principal and asking him or her if you can sponsor a specific activity that you have preselected. This may protect you from having to say yes to the sponsorship of an activity that you wouldn't really like to sponsor.

I once went to the principal of the middle school where I began my teaching career - I had a request to make. I told him that I liked debating activities and to please think of me for a future sponsor. The next term I got the job. It turned out to be the most rewarding experience at the school. Our debate team got on a local television station and we did well in competition with other schools.

2.   Get to know the principal.

Getting to know the principal can be advantageous for you. You can get to know the principal by acquainting him or her with the best work of your students - work that is above the average of the class.

The principal, if he or she knows something about you, can write important recommendations for your career advancement. I used my principal's recommendation to get into a Harvard summer session for secondary school teachers. True, I needed more than his support but it didn't hurt me to have it. His recommendation was typed on special school stationery with the school seal and all those little touches that are impressive.

3.   Communicating with a busy principal.

Rather than waiting to see the principal regarding a concern, write a note and leave space for a response. Suggest a time you can meet if he or she wants to discuss the concern. Make a copy of the note.

4.   Get to know the head counselors or deans.

The head counselors or deans <u>deal</u> with behavioral problems of students. They are the ones who determine and administer the appropriate punishment.

The head counselors or deans are among the most important teacher support people in the school. By maintaining on-going contact with them you'll keep up-to-date on what behavioral problems are appearing among many of the students. However, do not bother them with the minor problems that you can solve with the student's and/or their parents. To many referrals to the head counselors or deans can result in a delay.

TEACHER AND COMMUNITY RELATIONS

The school where you teach is part of a community. Many schools serve as community centers during non-school hours. If you learn about the school community and even participate in community affairs, you'll be better prepared to teach your students.

1.   Join some key organizations.

>   A note of caution; I would use a "wait and see" approach to joining teacher organizations. If you find only a small percentage of teachers are members of an organization, and they are viewed adversely by the school administrators, you may want to think twice before joining.

>   Consider joining professional organizations in your subject area and one or more general professional organizations, such as the National Educational Association, the American Federation of Teachers, etc.

>   Membership in professional organizations in your subject area, or areas, will introduce you to teachers in other districts and other states as well. You will find that the exchanges of ideas among members in these organizations will help you in teaching your subject.

>   Conventions held by professional organizations introduce teachers to new ideas and new techniques of teaching in a specialized discipline.

>   General organizations for teachers are important in establishing career standards, putting pressure on local, state and national politicians for improvements in education and in providing security for teachers threatened with legal action, medical catastrophes or other misfortunes.

>   As individuals we are weak and vulnerable. As part of an organization, we gain strength.

2.   Get acquainted with the politicians in your school's community.

>   Get to know as much about your local political leaders as possible. They can provide you with many benefits. You will get to know quite a bit about your school's community by all the information politicians (or their offices) have at their fingertips.

>   Politicians will usually make themselves available for occasional classroom visitations. They can often be persuaded to talk about major community problems that might interest the students.

3.   Get acquainted with local business people.

>   Local business leaders may be willing to support (money, time and/or service) several school programs. You could try to get some to sponsor a class. This would provide you with that little extra help that can make a big difference in the education of your students.

>   Visitations by business leaders can be an aid to career education for your students.

4.   Get acquainted with representatives of your local news media.

If you become known by representatives of the local news media you may be able to get in a few plugs for your special projects involving your students. Save any articles in the local newspaper in which you are featured for inclusion in your resume.

5.   Get to know the occupations represented within your school community.

Knowing the occupations within the local community can be of great use to you. When you are looking for good places for field trips, consider visiting local factories, farms and/or businesses. Representatives of occupational groups can often be taped for classroom visitations.

6.   Actively support local school bond issues.

Be an example to your students by participating in local affairs. Do not be afraid to ring doorbells and talk to people in the street about school bond issues. This gives you a chance to counter the all too frequent negative images of schools held by some people in many communities. You can inform people of the positive things going on in your school.

7.   Be careful of your behavior in the community where you teach.

You may not know it but many people place teachers on the same pedestal as priests, ministers and rabbis. Most communities demand the highest moral standards of their teachers. Why? Perhaps it has a lot to do with the role you play as an instructor of young children. People are generally quite protective of youth. If you violate community standards of conduct, you could find yourself being discussed in parent groups. Administrators might get complaints from parents and people in the community. As a beginning teacher you don't want this to happen.

8.   Get to know the police officers in your school community.

Police officers know a lot about what's going on with many of the students in your school. The police can tell you about substance abuse and other problems that face many of today's youth. In your conversations with police officers you'll be able to pick up many ideas that can be included in your lesson plans for almost any subject. The police are usually quite willing to visit your classes to make presentations on crime topics and street law.

SOME COMMON FEARS AND CONCERNS OF BEGINNING TEACHERS

A group of approximately 50 students studying to be teachers in a large urban comprehensive university were asked to list their major fears and concerns about their approaching first days in teaching. Three by five cards were handed out to the soon-to-be teachers and within five minutes the cards were completed and returned. Names were not required and I feel I got their honest feelings because of the quickness of their response and also the anonymity allowed. <u>Those fears/concerns and my responses are listed below</u>. My responses are based on the experience I obtained from over 30 years of classroom teaching in the public schools of California at the secondary level, and in the courses in curriculum and instruction which I taught at the college level for preparing students for the teaching experience.

FEAR/CONCERN (Subject Matter)

> Not know the content well.
> Having inadequate understanding of an issue - not being able to come up with good answers or explanations.
> I'm concerned that I won't have mastered my subject area content - that I won't be prepared enough as I begin teaching.
> My biggest fear is that I won't have anything to say.
> Not knowing the answers to student's questions.
> Remembering names and dates.
> I fear not having a full body of knowledge to teach 5+ different classes. Discipline and public speaking don't scare me, just the thought that I might not know enough to teach.
> Inadequate knowledge base.
> Not knowing enough.
> I'm most afraid of not knowing enough about the subjects I may have to teach. I fear kids will ask questions I cannot answer or that I will run out of things to discuss/study.
> Insufficient knowledge of a particular subject.
> Will not have the answer to a question.
> Fear of my own ignorance on any of a number of topics.
> Not being competent enough in my subject matter.

RESPONSE

> Regardless of what subject you teach, you probably know more about it than you think. You must remember that your students generally have little knowledge about any subject in the school curriculum.
>
> With your experience as a college student, you can quickly scan a few textbooks in any subject and amass enough factual material to seem well prepared in front of the class, even though you may not have had any formal instruction in the subject yourself.
>
> When I had to teach a course in which I had no background, a colleague came to the rescue. She laid out a course outline, listed some projects for students to do and gave me enough pointers to start me out. That course was one of my best teaching experiences because I did much better than I ever dreamed possible and I gained much knowledge new to me, as well as confidence in myself.
>
> You can get help from a department head and your colleagues who have taught the course you feel insecure about teaching.

A teacher is not required to be a walking encyclopedia of names, dates and facts. Knowing where to locate information is the best skill a teacher can have and a good skill to pass on to students.

Most student questions on a given topic follow the "5 W's and an H" pattern, that is Who?, What?, When?, Where?, Why? and How? If answers are not found in the textbook and you don't know the answers either, encourage your students to research the answers to their questions in the classroom or school libraries.

FEAR/CONCERN (Control of classes)

Discipline.
Keeping class disciplined without being a jerk.
Maintaining discipline.
Maintain interest - discipline.
Discipline will be a problem.
How to positively handle discipline problems; not just oust them but bring them into learning circle.
Classroom management (discipline-wise)
Maintaining a healthy learning environment and keeping discipline.
Establishing rapport - keeping control.
Dealing with the disruptors.
I might have some really disruptive kids in a class, which would make it difficult for me to concentrate.
Will a class eat me alive.
Sarcasm from students.
Disruptive, apathetic kids.
I'm afraid of losing control of the class. That my ways of disciplining will break down and no longer be effective.
Fear of losing/not gaining control of class.
My ability to maintain discipline in way I am happy with, and the students understand.
Will not know how to handle a particular student. (A personality conflict.)
Lack of attention.
Feeling intimidated by the students.
Classroom management.
Problems with classroom management interfering with teaching subject matter.
Can't control class.
Effective discipline.
Discipline problems.
Maintaining control in a classroom where I am not the most imposing physical being is of concern to me.
Not being aware of subtle classroom dynamics.

RESPONSE

First, students are easier to control if they have a clear idea of what you expect of them. Students usually want a teacher to have good class control. An undisciplined class is one that wastes everybody's time.

Control of a class is not based on physical force, but on mutual agreement between the teacher and the students. That agreement is that they are all engaged in a common cause - that of learning. Anything that obstructs that cause must be removed. This means establishing a few rules of behavior (see CLASS RULES form) and enforcing them.

I believe that class control depends mainly on the teacher being prepared, being well organized and being able to use a variety of techniques to control student misbehavior. Being prepared means having lessons and activities that cover the allotted time for class. It means having a clear idea of just what you want to accomplish in a given class. It also means having all the supplies and equipment necessary to carry out your teaching goals for the your classes. Being prepared helps to prevent the emergence of sarcastic, disruptive inattentive, apathetic, etc., students.

Being well-organized means having your seating charts in order, the grade book complete and forms such as passes in sufficient supply. The better organized you are, the less time you will have to spend on discipline; if you are not well organized, you will probably find that you are spending more time disciplining than instructing your students. It's a simple formula.

Using a variety of techniques to control student misbehavior allows you to have graduated responses to problems. In most cases, you can talk to a student and get him or her to stop behavior that you find objectionable. If the bad behavior continues, a reprimand that includes a warning may be in order. If this doesn't work you have to record the student's behavior and the counselor might be contacted so that another adult authority can talk to the student. If this doesn't produce results a formal referral to the appropriate dean is in order. A parent conference at school might do some good. At this conference every effort should be made to rehabilitate the student and bring him or her back to the classroom with a better attitude towards learning. If the problem with the student continues, however, a transfer to another class or even suspension from school might be called for.

If a student is intimidating you, or if you find you have a personality conflict with the student, you may have to skip over the control techniques and go directly to the counselor or appropriate dean.

Students are a little fearful of the teacher on the first day of class. After a little time the students will begin to test your limits. They want to find out just what you will or won't tolerate. This period of testing calls for you to be strict and quickly respond to any lapses in good behavior among your students.

There are several things you can do to keep problems from occurring. Having lots of work for students to do keeps most of them busy so that the unruly ones are easy to spot and can be disciplined while the others are working. Be on patrol in your classes. As a peripatetic pedagogue, you can monitor your students directly. However, even after you have done these things, you will usually still have some problems of misbehavior to contend with.

FEAR/CONCERN (Coping with too little time and too many students)

> Having too many students to follow-up, conference, refer.
> Having time for all the students.
> Grading all those papers.
> Being prepared for so many classes.
> Fear of not being able to reach many of students in class that size.
> Adequate prep time.
> Lack of time to teach (1 hr./1 yr.).
> Lack of time to prepare (prep/home).
> Preparation time/lesson plans.
> Running out of time to plan, to teach, etc., with increasing class sizes.
> Not enough time each day to develop lessons for a variety of classes on the following day.
> I'm concerned that I'll be so overwhelmed with work - grading papers, etc. - that I won't be able to teach in the depth (and test in the depth) in which I would like to teach.
> Not getting to know students individually.

<u>RESPONSE</u>

Generally it's better to cover a few topics well than to try to cover everything in a short span of time. If you are up against time limits, then you'll have to use your ability to decide on what is most important to teach. A real knowledge of a subject is demonstrated by what you can omit without serious loss to the students. Ask other teachers what they do about the time problem if you feel unsure about it.

When you have a great number of students to deal with, you may have to rely on the textbook which has lessons and exercises already prepared for student use. This will help reduce the time required to prepare for your classes.

When you get overloaded with students you have to make some changes in your teaching strategy. You may have to use more objective tests and assign fewer essay questions. To give attention to individual students you may want to organize a student-teacher corps. Use some of your best students as teaching assistants in your classroom. I used teaching assistants to take some students aside for individual help. The assistants can reach some students and produce dramatic changes in the academic performance of slow learners. Teaching assistants can help correct student tests and assignments, record grades and lighten the burden of too many students in many ways.

<u>FEAR/CONCERN (Dealing with physical violence in the classroom)</u>

Physical altercations.
Kids a lot bigger than me - drugs, gangs.
I'll get knifed my first day.
Violent kids.

<u>RESPONSE</u>

Prevention should be your goal when focusing on violence in your classroom. Such practices as keeping your students busy, with something to do at all times, will go far in limiting outbursts of violence. There are times, however, when nothing you do can prevent violent behavior in one or more of your students. What to do?

First you should try to cool down the violent student or students in a non-confrontational manner without taking sides or scolding. Do not accuse or use overly harsh words. Usually students don't want to do battle in a classroom and your appeals to reason will generally calm things down. If gentle persuasive conversation fails to work you may need to call for help. Hopefully, at the start of the term you made contacts with fellow teachers in adjoining classrooms so that you could agree to call on each other for quick help in an emergency. Calling the office will usually get you a response that is too late to do much good. In any event, the office should be contacted immediately if only to record the incident. As a last resort, do what you would do on the street; defend yourself as well as you can. Whatever the outcome, be sure to write up a complete report on the incident while it is still fresh in your mind. Make enough copies to be able to keep one for your own records.

There are some things beyond your control. Students on drugs and students involved in gang disputes are extremely difficult to deal with. If such students begin disturbances in the classroom or in the hall, you must immediately call the appropriate deans. Even if nothing is happening but you have suspicions of forthcoming troubles, notify the head counselors or deans. You should also spread the word among your neighboring teachers to keep on the alert. This is good insurance that you won't be caught in a violent situation without help readily available.

FEAR/CONCERN (Giving students individual attention)

> I guess I'm afraid of not being able to reach and interest so many different individuals.
> Being able to give enough attention to each student (in and out of class).
> That I won't be able to provide enough individual attention.
> Being able to get to know 150 - 200 students without becoming <u>too</u> distant or disconnected or emotionally drained.

RESPONSE

To give students individual attention means you have to make some time for them. You can't be lecturing or using visual aids in most of your class sessions and expect to give many students individual attention. You have to assign work to a class as a whole or divide up your class into groups that will work cooperatively on assigned tasks. Having done this you can walk up and down the aisles of the classroom or visit each of your working groups of students. In this way you'll have some time to contact a student on a one on one basis.

If you can, you should have a little time set aside before or after school when students can come to you for help and/or advice. Be sure the students are aware of this. You can post the times you are available on a class bulletin board, or you may wish to write the information in a corner of the blackboard. Setting aside a little time on two or more days a week may improve student performance in your classes.

It might be rewarding for you to ask your department head about a team teaching arrangement with another teacher in your department. In team teaching you can give considerable attention to each student while you share formal teaching duties with your colleague.

I found that one way to give more individual attention to students was to send a few groups of four or five students to the library to work on research assignments. With a smaller class size remaining, it was relatively easy to spend a little time with each student. I was careful to do this infrequently so as not to upset the school librarian unduly.

When you have students with varied interests you can appeal to each of those interests by assigning research projects that let the students work on topics of their choice within a broad subject area in the course. In this way you can keep your students' interest at a high level.

FEAR/CONCERN (Keeping students interested)

> Fear that I'll be the only one genuinely enthused about subject matter.
> My ability to provide a constant level of interest on the part of the students.
> Maintaining their interest and keeping the class together (not going too fast or too slow).
> Ability to keep them interested for a full hour.
> Keeping students interested.
> Keeping the students interested in the subject matter.
> Incorporating the lectures/presentations to be given to the class without losing everyone's interest in the subject matter.
> Whether or not I can keep a class interested or help them learn.
> Keeping the students interested in the subject matter.
> I won't be able to motivate them.
> Motivation/interest students.
> Not being able to motivate the students.

Motivating students.
How to motivate for the entire 50 minutes.
No one will listen.
That they'd rather be anywhere but in my class.
Students getting bored and reacting either passively or actively.
That I will be boring and kids will not pay attention, resulting in their not learning anything.
That I will not be creative enough.
Fear of boring students.
I'm also afraid that I'll be boring.

RESPONSE

Students generally have a very short attention span. There are many theories of its cause but nobody disputes its reality. With this knowledge you can design teaching strategies that will help to hold the interest of your students.

One strategy is to direct students in their work but to insist that they do the work. Most students don't like to passively listen to a teacher lecture them on a given topic. It's best to have them using their hands whenever possible. Making charts, maps, graphs, posters, collages and models are activities that help keep students awake.

Try giving students an in-class break. Let them stand and perhaps stretch alongside their desks for a minute to get their circulation going. This refreshing pause might help them keep their minds on their tasks.

The key thing to remember is to provide variety in the work presented to students. Variety can occur in two ways. First, vary your daily lesson plan. For example, you can divide a classroom period into time segments during which different activities can be carried out. Lecturing for a few minutes could be followed by a brief textbook exercise, which could be followed by a brief discussion, which could be followed by a library assignment, etc. Second, variety should be built into each individual activity. For example, in showing films to a class in U. S. History, don't show war films exclusively. In your film presentations, cover political, economic and social events in as balanced a way as you can.

Another strategy is to use current events whenever possible. The local newspapers and national news magazines are great resources for classroom use in both reading and writing assignments. You can tape television news and documentary programs for use in your classes.

Besides teaching strategies, there is the influence of your behavior on the students to consider. If you show an interest in what you are teaching it often rubs off on your students. You'll be surprised how your enthusiasm can motivate students!

It is unlikely that your entire class will be lacking interest in the subject. It is not always easy to determine how interested students really are in a subject. One way to sample student interest is by use of a short essay assignment.

The essay assignment is also a way to determine if you have been teaching the material too fast for the students to properly assimilate it. If you have been teaching the material too slowly you will undoubtedly observe a high level of student exasperation that will help you to gauge the proper teaching speed. In all of this try to avoid extremes of either teaching to the advanced students or the slower students exclusively while ignoring the needs of the average student in the class.

FEAR/CONCERN (Having students with a wide range of abilities in the same class)

> Dealing with a slow student.
> How to keep low achievers from falling out of the system altogether.
> I fear losing some of the less motivated kids while going in depth for interested students.
> Dealing with a very bright student.
> Afraid of inability to keep advanced students challenged without alienating slower students.

RESPONSE

You may have a class in which your students have a wide range of academic abilities. Teaching such a class is far from easy but not impossible. Teaching to the middle will only satisfy that portion of the class that we might call average students. It confuses the slower learners and bores the higher achievers. If the middle group is the largest group in the class, you may have to slant most of your work to that group, but you should have supplementary assignments that meet the needs of the other groups.

It is very difficult to issue different sets of textbooks. Such a practice means having different assignments, tests, discussions, etc. Also, students may feel embarrassed to be issued the "simple" textbook. You can issue all students the same textbook but have advanced supplementary textbooks available for those who want them.

When you make up your examinations you can present questions of various levels of difficulty from the quite simple to the quite complex. Students should be allowed to make a choice as to which questions they choose to answer. You could present five questions and each student would be required to answer any two of the five. Sometimes a challenge helps some students to reach a higher level of performance than they might have without a challenge.

One good strategy is to use the most academically capable students to help the slower learners in the class. This can be done in a group work setting where the help can be given in a fairly subtle way.

Having students work on a project in common can help to draw strength from various ability levels. I recall having one of my English classes following through on an idea they had to write and produce an original school musical of their own creation to be put on for the entire student body of the school. The best students in composition wrote various stories which were then evaluated by myself and some colleagues in music and drama. After one story was selected, the students learned how to write a script with help from the drama teacher. After school, groups of students worked on stage sets and props. There were enough parts in the musical to use the talents of every student in the class. One lesson was learned by all the students - everyone has a contribution to make in any united effort.

FEAR/CONCERN (Preventing teacher burnout)

> Keeping my enthusiasm and energy level up.
> Being "on" all the time.
> Repetition of the same class over and over.
> Burn-out/exhaustion/physical difficulties (too much coffee).
> Being exhausted.
> That I can maintain the level of enthusiasm I now have for teaching in the future.
> That I'll be exhausted by their energy and will burn-out.
> Fear of boredom in both myself and my students.
> Fear of burning out.
> Not being able to maintain a consistent level of energy.
> How to motivate when you're tired. What if the students don't seem to share your enthusiasm for a topic? Does that deflate you?

RESPONSE

There are many ways to try to prevent teacher "burnout". One of the most important ways is to be a little easy on yourself. Overwork is a prime cause of "burnout". It's been said elsewhere in this book but it bears repeating; if anyone should be slightly overworked, it should be the students, not you.

You can't put everything you've got into each class you teach on a daily basis. You probably won't survive what should be a long and rewarding career in education.

To keep your enthusiasm and energy level up you should keep yourself as healthy as possible. Make sure that your diet is a healthful one and that you exercise on a regular basis. Doing these things will help to make you more energetic in doing your work.

Besides overwork there are other factors involved in teacher "burnout". It can get pretty boring if you do the same things over and over again. A little variety in your teaching can perk you up. The variety of approaches to teaching subject matter is so great that you should be able to avoid being stale in your instruction. If you find that you rely to a considerable extent on the lecture method, try switching to a group work approach. If you normally stress textbook work, try switching to projects involving a considerable amount of library research. Another good way to enliven your course is to take your students on a field trip. Field trips will often help you more than the students!

On vacations, don't take your job with you in your suitcase. Force yourself into new experiences whenever possible. Many businesses make arrangements with school districts to give summer employment to teachers. The experiences the teacher receives in the business world can be quite refreshing and can help the teacher expand his or her vision beyond that of the small world of the classroom. Even an involvement in a non-teaching school activity, like sponsoring a club, can help to revive you. When things really get stale for you it may be time to ask for a transfer to a new school or a different grade level.

As your career develops, be sure to collect and save all awards, prizes, certificates, letters of commendation and recommendation, etc. An ego enhancing review of your educational accomplishments and successes can help keep you going in your career - it's quite therapeutic.

FEAR/CONCERN (Being prepared)

Students consistently failing tests or doing poorly on homework.
Being ill-prepared.
Coordinating process and content.
That a well planned lesson would be a flop and would fail to keep the students interested.
That I'll be stuck with textbooks I hate.
Grading subjective tests fairly.
What criteria to use to grade to be fair and know something was learned.
Ability to be discursive if needed and still maintain on schedule.
Promote sufficient discussion.
Appearing calm when I really don't know what I'm doing.
Being properly polished on all the lessons, everyday. I feel the teacher should be an expert on what he is teaching, at all times.
Staying focused on my topics for the lesson of the day.
That there will be kids I don't like and I will let this get in the way of teaching.
Maintaining a fresh and interesting approach for each class.
Not run out of subject material.
I'll plan a lesson and it won't be long enough, etc.

Planning lesson plans that are too long or too short, too simple, too complex.
Lacking a proper lesson plan.
To be prepared with enough material.
Fear of not having something to do everyday.
Running out of things to do, being unprepared.
Fear of not being able to come up with class ideas.
Will not have a lesson plan to fill out a full hour. (Run out of material).
That I don't know how long things should/can take and will totally misjudge time.
Not being able to come up with new angles on a set lesson plan that bombs with the kids.
Being unable to pronounce many of the multi-cultural names on the role sheets.
Remembering everyone's name.
Forgetting names.
Talking "above" the students' heads.
Becoming monotonous.

RESPONSE

Be prepared and you'll be in control of events in your classroom. Concerns in this category can be eased by having a check list of things to do and have ready as you begin teaching on the first day of the week.

First, have a weekly calendar big enough to make notations. On this calendar you should record your teaching plans for the week, your assignments (listed by textbook page number), and extra assignments which will give you some leeway if the students finish their work more quickly than you planned. Make notes on the calendar as to what actually happened and save the calendar for future reference. This way you won't be caught off guard.

As a beginning teacher it is very easy to misjudge time. This is where a well-planned calendar can be of help. The exercises you weren't able to have the students do on a particular day can either be assigned as homework or carried over to the next day's plan. You might want to underscore the assignments to which you give the highest priority so you will be sure that at least those assignments will be done by the students. The assignments not underscored can be considered to be expendable for the time being.

Secondly, have a seating chart with the students' names and their phonetic spelling in parentheses. This way their names can be called out the way the students want them pronounced. You can study the chart and memorize names while the students are doing a reading or writing assignment.

Don't be reluctant to use the textbook, even if you don't like it, for a start. Later you can use other resources and put less emphasis on the textbook if you wish.

Students are unlikely to flunk your first tests if those tests are solidly based on the textbook and the students know exactly what they are responsible for knowing.

Believe me, you'll be happy in your work if you are well prepared. In fact, if you get the students to work with their textbooks, you'll have some time to work on interesting lessons to reinforce the students' understanding of the subject.

When in your opinion a lesson fails and is just not making it with the students, it is vital to have contingency plans. You should immediately assign some textbook work and use the time provided to think up some new angles you may want to try the next day. Don't worry about a lesson that fails - it happens all the time and shouldn't discourage you from trying new approaches in the teaching of your subject.

Grading subjective work such as essays is not as difficult as you might think. A good approach is to have several categories in which to evaluate the student. See the example of grading an essay in the SAMPLE FORMS section of this book for further explanation.

It is often difficult to promote discussion among students in class. The best way to try is to formulate and ask good questions. Recall questions will not encourage discussion. You have to ask questions that force students to evaluate an issue. When they have to think of what is good or bad about something, or who is right or wrong and why, you are more apt to get exchanges of opinion among the students. Asking students how they feel about something is a way to draw some of the shy students out.

While we are on the subject of discussion, you should interrupt your lecturing from time to time to ask your students if they know the meanings of some of the words you are using. If students seem to be ignorant or confused on some of the meanings of the key words in your lecture, you're probably a bit over their heads. You can redesign your lecture based on the feedback you get from the students. It might be wise to make up a vocabulary list of key terms in your lecture and go over them with the students before you deliver any lecture to them.

To have fresh material each day requires some resource building on your part. You should have a file cabinet at home in which you have sections corresponding to the subjects that you teach. Whenever you see a passage in a book that is interesting and in your field, copy it down and file it. If you have a magazine or newspaper article of interest, cut it out and file it. Any interesting ideas you see on a television presentation can be summarized on a piece of paper and filed. If you obtain lesson plans from teachers at your school or other schools, file them also. In this way you'll have the material you'll need to maintain the interest of your students in the subjects that you teach and avoid monotony on your part.

If you expect to be able to discipline your students you must first be able to discipline yourself. If you feel inadequate in the amount of self-discipline you possess, you may be able to find some self-improvement program at a local college. If you can control your emotions you'll be able to give the appearance of calmness in front of your students. This can be done by slowing down the speed at which you speak and eliminating any unnecessary body movements, such as waving your hands. Self discipline and control of the emotions will also help you deal effectively with students you don't like.

FEAR/CONCERN (Being creative)

Creative ideas - (not having enough).
Being creative enough.
Coming up with innovative ideas.
That I won't be able to make the material fresh and interesting.
Running out of creative approaches.

RESPONSE

There are two major ways to be creative in classroom teaching. One way is to struggle to come up with your own original ideas. This way is very difficult. An easier and more abundant source of creative ideas is found in the body of lessons already thought out and tested. Don't resist borrowing ideas from others. I always scanned several textbooks in a given subject and compiled a list of ideas, drawing from each of them.

One of your first stops for ideas should be the other teachers in your department. You should be able to pick up a lot of good ideas from them. Professional organizations in your teaching field are another good source of ideas for lesson plans. You might even go to other schools and meet your teacher counterparts for ideas sharing sessions.

One reminder, don't try to be too creative. There are many standard and routine lessons that are really effective in getting ideas across to students. These lessons may seem old and worn to you but your students, exposed to these lessons for the first time, may find them to be new and interesting.

FEAR/CONCERN (Personal)

I'm scared of not being happy.
I am worried that I won't help them sufficiently in supplying them with the skills and enthusiasm to be happy in life.
How to deal with personal concerns.
I'm scared of not being as good a teacher as I think I should be.
That I won't be able to convince the students that I can relate to their racial, sexual, economic differences, even though I feel I will be very effective.
Not making a difference.
Having relevant things to say.
Just being nervous speaking in public.
Making sure that the subject matter doesn't offend anyone.
Fear of freezing up.
Will get sick, faint in front of class.
Getting a job to begin with.
The mere fact of facing 30 students.
That I won't be able to diffuse their hostility to each other.
Fear that they'll find out I don't know very much; that they'll be busy testing, challenging me and I'll feel afraid of them.
That they'll be bored by what excites me the most.
That 30% or more will not learn anything but still be able to pass the class.
My biggest fear is having to wake up early in the morning every day.
My other biggest fear is being intellectually stifled by the administration, if I don't push the pop idea of the day.
It was the "democratic" mob that targeted Socrates the "Father of Western Civilization".
Following thoughts where they will go is always dangerous.
I'll stammer - not be able to communicate.
My mind will go blank.
I'll loose interest after a few weeks.
Stage fright.

RESPONSE

Fear can be a healthy emotion if it doesn't go too far in controlling your behavior. Without fear there is no courage. A person without fears does not have to struggle to overcome them and successfully meet challenges. Being human, we tend to exaggerate our fears of unknown events beyond what reason should lead us to do.

In a beginning teacher, having fears and concerns are good omens. They can be an indication that you really care about what you are doing. You should realize that your fears probably come from the high expectations you have for yourself. You are probably afraid that your actual and ideal performances will be too far apart. This shows a high degree of motivation to succeed in teaching and is a good sign.

You can be sure that you'll develop a high level of confidence in yourself with time, patience and experience. And the more confidence you have in yourself, the happier you will be. You will become a model for many of your students and your enthusiasm and happiness will quite often be transmitted to your students. In return, their enthusiasm will encourage you and it is doubtful your interest will wane.

There are several ways you can overcome your fears. First, you will be more in control of what happens in your classroom than you think. There's no hidden TV camera in the corner of the room and administrators rarely have the time to monitor what you are doing. Even if they did, they'd be there to help you.

Few administrators have either the time or the inclination to influence what is being taught by any teacher on the faculty. If you are indoctrinating, or presenting only one side of an issue, instead of teaching, you might get an adverse reaction from some of your students, colleagues, school administrators, district administrators, community groups and parents.

Following thoughts where they go can be one of the most exciting experiences you can have in a classroom as long as you exercise common sense. When you realize you are getting into dangerous territory, it is time to switch the subject and allow a cooling off period for the members of the class who are emotionally involved in the subject under discussion. This should be done well before the end of class. You can diffuse a considerable amount of student emotion on a controversial issue by getting them to express their opinions in writing.

There is no way to be totally sure that some subject matter won't offend someone. Much of what is taught in many subjects is controversial. One way to avoid offending any student is to be as neutral as possible. Deal in facts and suppress any desire you may have to give your personal opinion to your students. As a significant adult in the lives of your students, you should always try to educate and never indoctrinate. Incidentally, one of the best ways to relate to students of different backgrounds is to be firm in your discipline, friendly in your manner, and fair in any disputes that arise. Being fair can also include the manner in which you teach subject matter. You should always try to give a balanced presentation on major points of view on any issue in the subjects you teach.

When you have students who exhibit hostility towards each other, you have a king size problem on your hands. Even Nobel Peace Prize winners have had a hard time dealing with people who have a mutual hostility towards each other. You might try group projects in your class to get students of different backgrounds working together on common projects. Also, you might give lessons on some of the causes of intergroup conflicts and hatreds. Try to emphasize anything that unites your students such as their being members of a teenage group, their membership in a student body or their common likes or dislikes. In other words, stress the similarities rather than the dissimilarities. You might find that enlisting the aid of the counselor will be helpful in dealing with student hostility.

A strategy for combating fear is to just "jump into the water" and get busy. The busier you are, and the busier your students are, the faster you'll forget your fears. You will become less nervous and will find such things as speaking to your students relatively easy to do. Also, if you are busy you will not freeze up, get sick, stammer, have stage fright or faint in front of the class - there will be too many demands upon your time. Nor will you be excessively challenged and tested by your students as might be the case if you do not have them working. Even in a large class of 30 or more students, if everyone is busy things will usually go quite smoothly.

As far as the fear of not reaching all your students is concerned, you're not a superman or superwoman. If you do the best you can for the greatest number of your students, you've done a good job.

There is no way to know just how much or how little a student has learned. The student may not show by the spoken or written word that the course has had any influence on him or her, but years later the student may act in a way that reflects the influence of your teaching. You should keep this in mind whenever you give a courtesy passing grade to a student.

You, as a beginning teacher, are entering the teaching profession at a time when shortages of teachers are becoming a national crisis. Even if the teacher shortages are overcome, there will always be a need for new teachers somewhere in almost every state. Don't worry about getting a job, just do the best you can in your work; that is your real challenge.

FEAR/CONCERN (Dealing with parents)

Facing parents who don't support your approach.
Being able to deal with parents.

RESPONSE

If your way of teaching a subject is criticized by a parent, the best thing you can do is to present your reasons for teaching the way you do in a clearly thought out manner. If the complaining parent or parents remain unmoved in their objections, you might suggest a transfer of the student to another class. You might also consider asking for their patience. You can always suggest that it is good for a student to have different styles of teaching in his or her educational experience.

Dealing with parents is where being organized really pays off. Parents appreciate meeting a teacher who can present hard evidence of their son's or daughter's academic and behavioral performance in the classroom. Parents are usually very grade conscious and they like to know with some exactness the ranking of their child. If your grade book is complete and easy to read most parents are satisfied.

It is a wise policy to have a series of ideas on how a student can improve his or her academic performance or behavior in class. These ideas should be well thought out and presented clearly to the parents. Always leave the door of hope open for the student, but insist on one point - you don't give the student a grade, the student earns the grade that he or she receives from you. Parents must be told that it is the students who have the primary responsibility in establishing their school records. In addition, parents should be told what your expectations are for their child. You should discuss the class rules and make sure that the parents have a copy of them. This is your chance to enlist the aid of the parents in influencing your students.

If you really are having major problems with a student and need to confer with the student's parents, you may wish to have a witness from your faculty attend the meeting. A counselor would be a likely choice. To protect yourself further, always be sure to have a written record of any major meeting with parents. Have the date and time of the meeting, the name of the witness and a synopsis of the meeting in your record.

Personally, the responses I received from the class of teachers-to-be made me relive my days as a student teacher at what seems a century ago. I had been teaching for so long I guess I forgot what it was like when I started. I remember that almost all of my fears turned out to be groundless. The fears that became a reality were overcome within my first few years of teaching. I, and many like me, didn't have the good fortune of having a guidebook such as this pointing the way! Being prepared reduces fears.

I have not omitted any of the students' statements. I asked for an expression of fears and concerns about teaching from a group of students who truly have them, and I hope I have set most of those fears to rest.

There are two key ideas that I would like to leave in the minds of future teachers. One is an old saying among generations of educators, "Keep them busy or they'll keep you busy". The other idea was brilliantly stated by the late Franklin D. Roosevelt, President of the United States, "You have nothing to fear but fear itself".

CLASS RULES

Class rules will give you, the student, a clear picture of what is expected from you here in school and in this class in particular. School is based on a "social contract". The most important item of this contract is that you, the student, bring to class a willingness to cooperate, to learn, and to study. The following are the "do's" and "don'ts" basic to behavior in a secondary school class.

1. Attendance

    You are expected to attend class everyday.

    A. Absence

       When you are absent from school, you are required to bring a note from home on your first day back. If you do not, it is an unexcused absence.

       Five days of unexcused absence in a term will result in a failing grade in this class.

       Tardy is being late for class. You are expected to have a pass or note from an accepted source, such as an administrator, teacher, counselor or a parent or guardian. If you have such a pass or note, this tardy will not be marked on the attendance report. (See C below.)

       If you are tardy and do not have a pass or note, I will hand you an Unexcused Tardy Report Form when you enter the classroom. If you complete this form and return it to me, I will mark you "tardy" on the attendance form. If you do not complete the form, this tardy will be marked as an unexcused absence.

       Three unexcused tardies will equal one unexcused absence. (Note: Five unexcused absences will result in a failing grade.)

    B. Extended absence

       If you are going to be out for an extended period of time, (a week or longer), it is the responsibility of you or your parents to contact the school to get the assignments that you are missing. Do NOT return after an extended absence and expect to be given all your assignments automatically.

    C. .Get a pass if you are going to be late for class

       If you are delayed by a teacher, counselor, etc., it is your responsibility to get a pass from the person detaining you.

2. <u>Make up work</u>

   If you have been absent, you should request make up work. The work will be given at a time convenient for me…NOT DURING CLASS. Make up work that is assigned must be turned in on the date set, otherwise it is unacceptable.

3. <u>Leaving the room</u>

   The passing period is the time to get a drink of water, use the rest room, get materials from your locker, etc. Do not request to leave the room unless it is a real emergency.

4. <u>Assignments</u>

   Assignments are given on a regular basis. They are designed, in many cases, to take time outside of class.

   You have reached the point in your education where school is going to interfere with your other activities. To be successful in school you are going to have to regard school work as your main activity - even at the expense of your job, social life, sports and family activities.

5. <u>Late work</u>

   Work turned in late will be accepted, but there is no guarantee it will be given credit.

6. <u>Help</u>

   If you need help, please contact me before or after school.

7. <u>Behavior</u>

   Listed below are some examples of proper behavior and some types of behavior that will not be tolerated.

   A.   Be on time and preferably in your seat and working when the bell rings.
   B.   .If you are tardy, either present your teacher with a tardy pass or pick up an Unexcused Tardy Report Form from the teacher to be completed and returned at the end of class. Then take your seat without creating any further disturbance.
   C.   Have your materials (paper, pencil, textbook, etc.) with you.
   D.   .Do not work on assignments for other classes in this class.
   E.   Raise your hand if you wish to speak to answer or ask a question.
   F.   Follow directions and instructions.
   G.   Do not shout out the door or window to a friend.
   H.   Do not go to the door or window to speak to a friend.
   I.   .Do not bring food or drinks to class.
   J.   Gum. You may chew as long as you don't crack, snap, pop, etc. Don't leave it under a desk or chair.
   K.   Please do not ask to "borrow". It is your responsibility to bring your own materials.
   L.   You are responsible for returning all materials issued by the school in good order. You will have to pay for damaged or lost items.
   M.   When the teacher or anyone else is talking, you should be silent.
   N.   Radios and tape players should be left at home. If you bring them to class, you and the article will go to the head counselor or dean. Cell phones should be turned off.
   O.   Hats. You are to remove your hat when entering the room.
   P.   Items that are a disturbance will be sent to the head counselor or dean. Examples of things that disturb the class are radios, toys, weapons, noisemakers, skateboards, etc. You must retrieve them from the head counselor or dean.

8. Referral (to the head counselor or dean)

> If for some reason you are referred to the head counselor or dean, you cannot return to class until I have received a copy of the referral from the head counselor or dean.

9. Grades

> Grades are a composite of all your work, or expected work, during a report period. Semester grades are an average of the report periods. No passing grade is given simply for attendance.

_____   _____
Date   Student Signature

_____   _____
Date   Parent(s) or guardian(s) Signature

STUDENT PROFILE

<u>IF THERE ARE ANY QUESTIONS OR CONCERNS</u> ABOUT RESPONDING TO ANY OF THE FOLLOWING ITEMS, PLEASE CONSULT WITH THE INSTRUCTOR.

Date:_____ Course Title:_____ Period_____

Instructor:_____

1. _____Names_____   2._____Phone Numbers_____
   First   Last   Home #   Work #

   Yours_____   _____

   Mothers_____   _____   _____

   Fathers_____   _____   _____

   Guardians_____   _____   _____
   (if applicable)

3. Your address_____

4. Grade level in school_____

5. Dominant language spoken at home_____

6. Other languages you speak with some fluency: A._____

   B_____ C_____ D_____

7. Previous schools attended: A._____ B._____

   C._____ D._____ E._____

8. Do you intend to continue your education after high school? _____

   If yes, which school(s) would you like to attend, or know you will attend_____

   _____

   If no, what specifically do you intend to do?_____

   _____

9. What kind of job would you like to have when you are

   A. twenty-five years old_____

   B. forty-five year old_____

10.   What are your leisure time activities, hobbies, etc._____

_____

11.   What newspapers, magazines, etc., do you read?

Daily_____

Weekly_____

Monthly_____

12.   What favorite television programs do you regularly watch?

_____

13.   Do you hold membership in any clubs or organizations?

_____

14.   What is your major (subject)?_____

15.   What do you think you will learn from this course?_____

_____

16.   In what school activities or groups are you active?_____

_____

17.   Are you interested in participating in student government at school? Yes_____ No_____

18.   Where else in the United States have you lived?_____

_____

19.   In what other countries have you lived?

A._____ How long?_____

B._____ How long?_____

C_____ How long?_____

20.   List all other courses you are taking this semester and the periods that you are taking them.

Course	Period	Course	Period
_____	____	_____	____
_____	____	_____	____
_____	____	_____	____
_____	____	_____	____

21. Do you ever think about taking on the same occupations of your parents? Yes___ No_____

    If yes, why? _____

    If not, why? _____

22. Do you have any brothers or sisters?_____ If yes, what are their names and ages?

    _____

    _____

23. What prizes and awards have you won?_____

    _____

24. What kinds of guest speakers would you like to have in this class? _____

    _____

26. How much time do you average each evening on the phone?_____

27. How much time do you average each evening on homework?_____

28. How much time do you average each evening watching television?

29. Do you work after school?_____ If yes, how many days and hours?

    (Circle days and list hours below each day.)
    Days: MON   TUES   WED   THURS   FRI   SAT   SUN

    Hours: _____   _____   _____   _____   _____   _____   _____

30. Do you engage in any after school activities?_____
    If yes, how many days and hours?
    (Circle days and list hours below each day.)
    Days: MON   TUES   WED   THURS   FRI   SAT   SUN

    Hours:_____   _____   _____   _____   _____   _____   _____

31. What books, if any, have you read in the past eight months which were not required reading for any school courses?

    A._____

    B._____

    C._____

THANK YOU FOR YOUR COOPERATION IN COMPLETING THIS PROFILE. PLEASE
FEEL FREE TO USE THE SPACE BELOW FOR ANY ADDITIONAL COMMENTS YOU
MAY WISH TO MAKE.

USING THE QUANTITATIVE ESSAY GRADING MATRIX

The Quantitative Essay Grading Matrix is a tool designed to help a teacher grade subjective essay examinations in a fair and balanced way. By having six criteria with which to evaluate a student's paper, a teacher can show a student and parent areas of strengths and weaknesses in a given written assignment. Through rewriting a student can be encouraged to overcome his or her weaknesses and become a better writer.

The maximum score possible for a student to achieve is 100 points. The lowest score possible would be 6 points. Such a low score would be a rarity indeed.

In each of the sections of the matrix, the higher the number of points circled, the better the student's score. By totaling the circled numbers in all six sections, an overall grade is determined. The following chart shows how the points can be used to assign a letter grade:

GRADING CHART

Points	Letter Grade
90 to 100	A
80 to 89	B
70 to 79	C
60 to 69	D
6 to 59	F

Note: I'm not suggesting you present each student with this form for every written assignment. But for two or three major essays in the term it would be most helpful to use the form.

NAME_____ PERIOD:_____

ESSAY SUBJECT:_____ DATE:_____

QUANTITATIVE ESSAY GRADING MATRIX

Essay responds to question? If not, essay cannot be graded. If yes, essay can be graded.

Weight	Criteria	Points
25%	Thesis well stated and appropriate to assignment	1 2 3 4 5 6 7 8 9 10 11 12 13 14 15 16 17 18 19 20 21 22 23 24 25
25%	Thesis well supported by reasons, examples, evidence, illustrations	1 2 3 4 5 6 7 8 9 10 11 12 13 14 15 16 17 18 19 20 21 22 23 24 25
25%	Organization (good introduction, body, conclusion)	1 2 3 4 5 6 7 8 9 10 11 12 13 14 15 16 17 18 19 20 21 22 23 24 25
15%	Grammar, spelling, punctuation	1 2 3 4 5 6 7 8 9 10 11 12 13 14 15
5%	Legibility	1 2 3 4 5
5%	Directions followed (written in ink, correct heading, etc.)	1 2 3 4 5

OVERALL GRADE

1	2	3	4	5	6	7	8	9	10
11	12	13	14	15	16	17	18	19	20
21	22	23	24	25	26	27	28	29	30
31	32	33	34	35	36	37	38	39	40
41	42	43	44	45	46	47	48	49	50
51	52	53	54	55	56	57	58	59	60
61	62	63	64	65	66	67	68	69	70
71	72	73	74	75	76	77	78	79	80
81	82	83	84	85	86	87	88	89	90
91	92	93	94	95	96	97	98	99	100

COMMENTS

_____

_____

_____

ANECDOTAL RECORD SHEET

Student's
Name_____

Date   Time   Description of Behavior

_____ _____ _____
_____ _____ _____
_____ _____ _____
_____ _____ _____
_____ _____ _____
_____ _____ _____
_____ _____ _____
_____ _____ _____
_____ _____ _____
_____ _____ _____
_____ _____ _____
_____ _____ _____
_____ _____ _____
_____ _____ _____
_____ _____ _____
_____ _____ _____
_____ _____ _____
_____ _____ _____
_____ _____ _____
_____ _____ _____
_____ _____ _____
_____ _____ _____
_____ _____ _____
_____ _____ _____
_____ _____ _____
_____ _____ _____
_____ _____ _____
_____ _____ _____
_____ _____ _____
_____ _____ _____
_____ _____ _____
_____ _____ _____
_____ _____ _____
_____ _____ _____
_____ _____ _____

PHONE CALL RECORD SHEET

DATE	TIME	CALL FROM/TO	SUMMARY OF MESSAGE/CONVERSATION

MISBEHAVIOR SLIP

Student's Name_____ Period:_____
                      (Last)   (First)

Date:_____ Time:_____

Rule violation:

___Late to class   ___Disturbing class

___Cut class   ___Fighting in class

___No book   ___Eating/Drinking in class
___No supplies

                                               ___Coming to class with unauthorized equipment,
                                                   such as skateboards, radios, etc.

Explanation:_____

Student's
signature:_____

Teacher's
signature:_____

Comments:_____

_____

_____

HALL PASS

<u>HALL PASS</u>

Period:_____

Name:_____
      (Last)   (First)

                    Time

Date: _____   Returned:_____

                    Time

                    Left:_____

Total time gone: _____

Destination:

___Rest room   ___Library
___Locker   ___Counselor
___Office   ___Other

_____
(Teacher's signature)

<u>HALL PASS</u>

Period:_____

Name:_____
      (Last)   (First)

                    Time

Date:_____   Returned:_____

                    Time

                    Left:_____

Total time gone   _____

Destination:

___Rest room   ___Library
___Locker   ___Counselor
___Office   ___Other

_____
(Teacher's signature)

<u>HALL PASS</u>

Period:_____

Name:_____
      (Last)   (First)

                    Time

Date:_____   Returned:_____

                    Time

                    Left:_____

Total time gone: _____

Destination:

___Rest room   ___Library
___Locker   ___Counselor
___Office   ___Other

_____
(Teacher's signature)

<u>HALL PASS</u>

Period:_____

Name:_____
      (Last)   (First)

                    Time

Date:_____   Returned: _____

                    Time

                    Left:_____

Total time gone: _____

Destination:

___Rest room   ___Library
___Locker   ___Counselor
___Office   ___Other

_____
(Teacher's signature)

BOOK LIST

SUBJECT_____ PERIOD_____

NAME OF STUDENT   BOOK NO.   CONDITION OF BOOK

UNEXCUSED TARDY REPORT FORM

PERIOD_____ DATE_____

NAME_____ TIME_____

REASON/EXCUSE/ALIBI for arriving late to class without a pass.
_____

_____

_____
Student Signature

Turn this form into the instructor at the end of class. If you don't, you will be charged with one unexcused absence rather than a "tardy". <u>Three unexcused tardies will be the equal to one unexcused absence (cut) and a "passing grade" cannot be given if unexcused absences exceed five days during the term.</u>

.- -
-

UNEXCUSED TARDY REPORT FORM

PERIOD_____ DATE_____

NAME_____ TIME_____

REASON/EXCUSE/ALIBI for arriving late to class without a pass.
_____

_____

_____
Student Signature

Turn this form into the instructor at the end of class. If you don't, you will be charged with one unexcused absence rather than a "tardy". <u>Three unexcused tardies will be the equal to one unexcused absence (cut) and a "passing grade" cannot be given if unexcused absences exceed five days during the term.</u>

SELECTED BIBLIOGRAPHY OF PROFESSIONAL JOURNALS

Note: These are just a few of many journals in the field of education. Most reference libraries have books that will refer you to periodicals and journals by subject.

AFT in the News - American Federation of Teachers. 555 New Jersey Ave., NW, NW Washington DC 20001

AICCT Journal - Assn. For the Improvement of Teaching. 9131 Fletcher Pkwy, Ste 124 LaMesa, CA 92041

ALAN Review - National Council of Teachers of English. 1 University Heights/UNCA. Asheville, NC 28804 (reviews and discusses adolescent literature)

ASTC Newsletter - Assn of Science-Technology Centers. 1413 K St. N.W., 10th Flr., Washington DC 20005 (about science education issues)

American Biology Teacher - Natl. Assn. Of Biology Teachers. 11250 Roger Bacon Drive, Reston, VA 22090 (biology curriculum matters)

American Education - U.S. Dept. Of Education. 400 Merlin Ave., S.W., Washington DC 20202

American Educator - American Federation of Teachers. 555 New Jersey Ave., NW. NW Washington DC 20001 (problems of teacher welfare, etc.)

American Journal of Physics - American Institute of Physics. 5110 Roanoke Pl., College Park, MD 20740 (physics instruction)

California English - California Assn. Of Teachers of English. 225 Calle de Sereno, Leucadia, CA 92024 (English matters K - 16)

Educators Guide to Free Filmstrips - Educators Progress Service, Inc., 214 Center St., Randolph, WI 53956 (filmstrips plus free items for teachers in many subjects)

Elementary /Economist - Joint Council on Economic Education. 2 Park Ave., New York, NY 10016-5601 (teaching activities for economics)

English Journal - Natl. Council of Teachers of English. 1111 Kenyon Rd., Urbana, IL 61801 (activities in teaching English)

Journal of Physical Education, Recreation and Dance
    American Alliance for Health, Physical Education, Recreation and Dance. 1900 Association Dr., Reston, VA 22091 (ideas on teaching in these subjects)

Journal of Reading - Intl. Reading Assn., 800 Barksdale Rd., Box 8139, Newark, DE 19714 (teaching reading at secondary level)

NABE: Journal of the National Association for Bilingual Education - Las Americas Publ. Co., 37 Union Square, W., New York. NY 10003

NEA Today - Natl. Educ. Assn., 1201 16th St., NW, Washington, DC 20036 (news, instructional trends, etc.)

School Arts Magazine - Davis Publications, Inc., 50 Portland St., Worcester, MA 01608 (activities in teaching arts and crafts)

School Science and Mathematics - School Science, Box 1614, Indiana Univ. of Pa., Indiana, PA 15705 (topics in high school mathematics and science)

School and Society - Society for the Advancement of Education, 1860 Broadway, New York, NY 10023 (current events in the whole field of education)

Science and Children - Natl. Science Teachers Assn., 1742 Connecticut Ave., N.W., Washington, DC 20009 (designed to meet the needs of middle school science teachers)

Science Education - John Wiley, 605 Third Avenue, New York, NY 10158 (trends in science instruction)

Social Education - Natl. Council for the Social Studies, 3501 Newark St. NW, Washington, DC 20016 (for teachers of Social Studies at all levels)

THE IMPACT OF COMPUTERS, VIDEOS, CELL PHONES AND THE INTERNET ON TEACHING AND LEARNING

INTRODUCTION

As the 21ˢᵗ century dawns we find ourselves in the midst of an unprecedented series of technological revolutions. The computer, videos, cell phones and the Internet are especially important in this information age.

Educators should anticipate developments and problems in the use of new technologies before they occur and changes should be managed as soon and effectively as possible. Some probabilities can be forecast already. The job market, for example, will increasingly demand that employees have computer literacy and they will look to the schools to provide trained personnel. Fields such as information technology, interactive multi media, education, nursing, medical arts, sales and marketing, real estate and restaurant management are just a few of the industries currently seeking computer literate workers. Who knows what new fields will mushroom in the future. It's safe to say that computer skills will be increasingly necessary for almost all occupations.

A probability that could become a major social problem is the trend towards a two tiered society of digital haves and have-nots.

The dispensing of teachers' knowledge is becoming somewhat eroded today. Students have all the information available on the Internet and mass media but they might not be able to interpret it correctly. The teacher's role will be to facilitate the educational advancement of the students by keeping them focused on issues, problems and topics appropriate to their courses of study. The student's academic skills should be stressed with special care given to alerting students to the need for examination of sources of information. Verification of the credibility of sources will be essential.

In the new learning environment, both teachers and students will see changes in their respective roles. Following is a list of comparisons of teaching and learning before and after the coming of the computer, the video, cell phones and the Internet and some of the possible new roles of teachers and students.

TEACHING AND LEARNING, THEN AND NOW: A COMPARISON

BEFORE THE COMPUTER, ETC

AFTER THE COMPUTER, ETC.

The teacher's authority in academic matters was generally unchallenged

The academic authority of the teacher is somewhat diminished by students having alternative authorities to investigate

Teacher's and student's roles were clearly differentiated

Teachers and students more like co-workers

The classroom was an isolated cell for learning

Interclass, interschool and international collaboration in the teaching and learning process

Teachers often imparted information to their students orally

Information on the Internet is a vast resource for students. Teachers begin to lose their knowledge monopoly

Textbooks played a big part in instruction

Textbooks are more supplementary and not so essential for learning

Education films tended to be years behind the times

Visual information on the Internet is quite current, far exceeding the ability of textbooks, reference works and films to keep up to date

Teachers could rely on low tech teaching tools

Teachers need more training in the use of high tech teaching tools

Reading and writing skills stressed

In addition to reading and writing skills, computer literacy is stressed

Opportunities for individualized instruction were extremely limited	Great opportunities to individualize instruction, e.g. in math slow, regular and fast learners can study at their own pace with the use of appropriate videos
Students were seldom involved in cooperative learning in pairs or groups	Students working in pairs or in groups is made easier by use of the computer. Students studying the same topic don't have to fight over one volume of an encyclopedia
Students were often passive with few chances for oral presentations to their classmates	Students are given great opportunities to take an active role in their own education through surfing the net
Students seldom had a wide range of choices of topics for study	Choices are all but unlimited
Students' academic performance was usually measured by quizzes, tests and occasional reports	Student's academic performance can be measured in many more ways, e.g. debates, discussions, group presentations, student made videos, skits, plays, displays, etc.
Students encouraged to follow directions, absorb instruction and complete assignments	Students encouraged to think critically, collaborate, communicate effectively and be self-reliant
The library is a repository of printed data for student retrieval	The library is a conduit to various databases of information
Students prepared for the industrial age	Students prepare for the information age

Teacher and student relationships rather exclusive. Relatively little parent and teacher interaction	Networking among parents, administrators, students and teachers amount to the creation of an academic village that broadens a students support group
Students and parents often surprised by report card grades	Students and parents have the possibility of knowing student grades on a daily basis. Surprises about grades should vanish
Home schooling programs limited the number of subject offerings that were possible	Modern media technology offers home school students a broad range of subjects, e.g. foreign language offerings can be greatly expanded
Little business involvement in schools	Much more business sponsorship in classroom activities
A lockstep time schedule to graduation	Some students finish high school in two years, others take five or six
Students grouped by age	Students grouped by interests and abilities
Students go to traditional large schools	Students grouped into learning families; charter schools proliferate
Students work by themselves	Students have mentors who guide their learning
Students spend most of their time in the schools	Much time spent outside of school in internship programs

POSSIBLE TEACHER AND STUDENT ROLES

Teachers will:

- Facilitate student project work taking care to keep students on task.

- Stimulate student interest in the various aspects of a given subject.

- Monitor student use of computers as well as their use of the Internet.

- Develop student skills to make optimum use of the great mass of information they'll have at their fingertips.

- Guide students in evaluating sources of information.

- Plan cooperative learning experiences.

- Encourage students as individuals or as groups to instruct their classmates in ways that make students teachers.

- Be on the alert for signs of medical problems that might result from excessive computer use by students.

Students will:

- Solve problems, explain how to do things, analyze topics and work on projects that sharpen synthesizing skills.

- Evaluate and review many sources of information.

- Participate in decision making in ways that allow students some choice within the prescribed curriculum.

- Research topics using the Internet as well as other sources

- Present debates, speeches, discussions and student made videos

- Create original skits, plays, poems, displays of artwork, miscellaneous displays and other creative works.

SUBSTITUTE TEACHING

1.   Absent teachers often expect substitute teachers to

- arrive at school at least 15 minutes ahead of time so there will be time to look over lesson plans, obtain any equipment such as television sets, overhead projectors, etc. There should also be time to deal with any problems that might arise.

- check the absent teacher's mailbox for important notices pertaining to the classes being covered. Do not open the absent teacher's personal mail!

- contact attendance clerks to see if attendance forms need to be printed.

- take roll carefully. Absences and tardies should be properly recorded.

- follow all given lesson plans completely and exactly.

- announce homework assignments to each class at the beginning and at the end of the period.

- maintain class discipline and send serious offenders to the office with a school referral form filled out as completely as possible.

- keep good housekeeping in the classroom and, if applicable, see that students place their chairs on the tables at the end of the teaching day so that floor cleaning is made easier for the custodial staff.

- make a record of all incoming telephone calls and put that record in the absent teacher's mailbox.

- collect all quizzes, tests and homework as requested and clearly identify the student work by period for the absent teacher.

- list names of especially cooperative and uncooperative students by class period and place the list in the absent teacher's mailbox.

- write a brief summary of how the classes went and place the summary in the absent teacher's mailbox.

2.   Substitute teachers often expect absent teachers.to

- provide full and adequate lesson plans for all classes.

- place all necessary information for the substitute teacher in a clearly marked folder placed prominently on the main classroom desk. The folder should contain lesson plans, a time schedule of classes, a list of faculty members and the subjects they teach, referral forms, attendance forms, etc. It would be helpful to include any rules of discipline being followed so that there will be no break in the enforcement of rules and regulations for students. A number 2 pencil should be provided if needed for filling out attendance forms.

- list at least two cooperative students in each class being covered so that they could assist the substitute teacher if such assistance is requested.

- list the names and room numbers of neighboring teachers who might help answer questions the substitute teacher might have.

- have emergency lesson plans in a place known by the school secretary who handles substitute teachers in case of accidents and other unexpected emergencies.

- provide information to the substitute teacher about any difficult students or classes. If any students have special medical needs or are on medications for behavioral problems, the substitute teacher should be informed.

- write a brief note of welcome and thanks to the substitute (guest) teacher.

Notes

Notes

Notes

Notes

Notes

<u>Notes</u>

<u>Notes</u>

<u>Notes</u>

<u>Notes</u>

Notes

<u>Notes</u>

Notes

<u>Notes</u>

Notes

Notes

<u>Notes</u>

Notes

<u>Notes</u>

About the Authors

Henry T. Conserva has taught in the public schools of California for over 50 years. He has been a curriculum specialist in social studies for the San Francisco Unified School District and has taught student teachers at San Francisco State University. He has done postgraduate study at Tel Aviv University in Israel and at Harvard's Japan Institute. He is the author of Earth Tales and Propaganda Techniques.

Ms. Jean F. Dewees has had a long career as an administrator in the Employee Relations Department in one of the Fortune 500 Companies. At Corporate Headquarters in San Francisco she gave formal instruction to many personnel in various departments. Lately, she has written and edited textbooks for grade school use. As an accomplished photographer, many of her photographs have been published in a California history textbook. She received her Bachelor of Arts degree from the University of California at Berkeley and she has studied at the City College of San Francisco, the University of Oregon, San Francisco State University and Santa Rosa Junior College.

Printed in the United States
27012LVS00001B/177

9 781410 763976